Stammer

DARREN BENHAM

Stammer

Regaining My Speech and My Life

DARREN BENHAM

ORPEN PRESS

Published by
Orpen Press
Upper Floor, Unit K9
Greenogue Business Park
Rathcoole
Co. Dublin
Ireland

email: info@orpenpress.com
www.orpenpress.com

Paperback ISBN 978-1-78605-071-7
ePub ISBN 978-1-78605-072-4

Printed in Dublin by SPRINTprint Ltd

For my children, my family and A.M.

Thanks for caring.

Acknowledgements

This book could not have been published without the hard work and dedication of Eileen O'Brien at Orpen Press. Thank you Orpen Press, and especially Gerry Kelly, for taking a chance on someone like me.

Peter O'Connell, literary agent – I still owe you a cup of tea. You saw something I had trouble believing existed.

Grainne Killeen, Killeen PR, many thanks for the hard work and advice, and for pushing me. No room for comfort zones.

Thanks to the teachers and staff at O'Connell Schools who taught me how to hurl and kick a ball, and who encouraged the kid from the inner city.

Thanks to all my former teammates and managers at Scoil Uí Chonaill GAA club. Thank you for sticking by me and for being there for me when times were difficult. I owe you guys more than I can ever repay. I wish there was twenty more years left in the legs.

To the DCU hurling teams of 1993–1997, surely there is another reunion match left in the tank? You guys are simply the greatest group of lads I've ever known. Thank you.

Thanks to everyone involved in the McGuire Programme who continue to assist in my ongoing recovery today. Joe O'Donnell and Robert O'Brien, I owe you two a huge debt of gratitude.

Brian Cornelia. We started together and you read the first drafts. Thanks. I wish I had half your courage.

JP Murphy – thanks for asking the right questions and being someone I aspire to be.

Paddy Moran, thank you for the education.

Da, thanks, you are the brightest man I know.

Ma ... thanks ... your 'sunshine'.

I want to thank my sisters for their ongoing support and for the memories we share.

Grace, I'm so proud of you.

To my extended cousins and relatives, this is the real me.

To my kids. I love you so much. I cannot wait to give a speech at your weddings.

To the extended Mueller clan, thank you for treating me like one of your own.

To Astrid ... for simply *everything*.

Contents

Preface

As a young boy, coming to terms with the realisation that speaking was going to be something I would have to battle with for the rest of my life, I felt helpless and entirely alone. My life at that time was utterly consumed with thinking about and reacting to stammering.

I wrote this book as a means of recording my ongoing personal journey but also for the fellow stammerers, the mothers and fathers of the children crying in their rooms, not knowing how to begin to tackle the seemingly insurmountable task of verbal communication. I know exactly how you feel and I think this book can be helpful to you because at the very least it tells you exactly how *not* to deal with the physical and mental aspects of chronic stammering. However, there is always time to do something about it.

I address other important themes like mental health, family issues and the necessity of surrounding yourself with support and encouragement. These themes are universal and important for us all to remember.

I mention several important relationships in this book, including my immediate family and my previous marriage. My family had a profound effect on me growing up and though I detail some tough times, I love and respect my father, mother and sisters for their collective guidance and encouragement. The events in the book shaped me and my view of the world and are documented to push the story and narrative forward in order to generate a greater understanding of what went on in my mind at that time. I have no hidden agenda.

Introduction

I have always struggled with my mental health. I endured a severe stammer as a child and as a result my whole consciousness was shrouded in darkness. I hated myself from an early age because I could not communicate verbally. I embarrassed myself every single time I tried to speak. It wasn't until I was almost 30 that I could say my name without chronic stuttering.

My childhood was fraught with tension and a pervasive anxiety. I felt unsafe and vulnerable for many years.

I expressed myself through Gaelic football and hurling, joining the Dublin senior hurling panel when I was 21.

When my marriage ended and I was separated from my children, I broke down psychologically. I was forced to confront my irrational behaviours and emotional instabilities and discovered the reason why, for me, life is sometimes very difficult and feels insurmountable. This discovery brought about a greater understanding of how my mind works and why I react to certain triggers like I do.

With the help of someone I love, I was able to confront issues that had festered for so long they had polluted my psyche. My negativity and depression made me so physically ill for such a long time that I believed I was going to live the rest of my life in pain.

My stuttering nearly destroyed me. A stammer will define and enslave you if you let it. If you face it, confront it, challenge it and demand more of your speaking itself, it will back down, it will turn away and hide, but never turn your back on it for a minute. Like the coward it is, it will rise up and stab you in the back when you least expect it.

By detailing the battles I have endured, I hope to be able to prove to you that there is hope when things appear to be at their darkest and you feel you cannot endure another day or another night of being alone with your thoughts and your broken mind.

Time does heal. The pain does fade. You will find love again. You will find answers. You just have to keep looking and believe.

1

Early Years

When I was a baby, my father, mother and I lived in a Dublin Corporation flat in Gardiner Street in north Dublin's inner city. I have some vague recollection of living there, of people and relatives visiting and everything appearing as a shade of brown, which was the fashion in the 1970s. When he was seventeen my father came to Ireland, ostensibly to get work but I discovered many years later because he was running away from his own troubles. My mother had left school at fourteen and married the first man she loved. She came from a traditional Catholic household with siblings all living within close proximity to each other in similar Corporation housing. It must have been some surprise to them being presented with a 6-foot-2 Protestant immigrant from Kent, England as a future son-in-law but they appeared to have managed regardless.

Photos of me at that time reveal a rotund and evidently happy young baby, devouring the milk and mash potatoes that my mother fed me. She was subsequently chastised by the local nurse who was astounded at how much I weighed. My mother ruefully put me on a diet less likely to progress me to morbid obesity. She was convinced in her naivety that I would obtain the best nourishment from milk and spuds and she was only trying to be the best mother she could be. Despite her good intentions, the muscles in my legs developed sufficiently to carry my oversized torso and, despite my early diet, I became an active and outgoing child.

I recall looking at pictures of my parents around that time in their various beige-coloured clothing and innocent smiles. My father was an imposing figure, tall, lean and evidently fit, accustomed to hard work. When he came to Ireland he principally sought work as a scaffolder, working on construction sites and buildings and erecting complex structures of steal lattices and girders. Apparently, he was very good at it too and was very much sought after by the relevant scaffolding companies in Dublin at that time.

I have hazy memories of the high ceilings in Gardiner Street, sunshine, noisy neighbours and linoleum flooring. My father brought me everywhere he went. Again, thanks to family albums, there are pictures of me sitting proudly on his broad shoulders with my unruly brown hair touching my eyes and covering my ears, a smile etched across my face oblivious to everything but the fact that I was with my father. I frequently went horse-riding with him and some of his friends (the pictures are there to prove it), which was not, needless to say, the typical pastime of Dublin inner-city residents at that time.

There was always a ball around the house or out the back somewhere and I remember swinging my chunky legs and using up all my concentration to make a connection and pass to my father. He was an avid follower of soccer and followed his boyhood team of Gillingham in Kent. I remember him watching the TV intently on a Saturday afternoon for the final soccer results, hoping his team would obtain those elusive points to languish ignominiously in mid-table of Division Three.

My eldest sister, Vicky, arrived eighteen months after me, something that evidently caused huge disruption in my young family but I have no recollection of being particularly perturbed about her arrival. I seemed to generate my own trouble.

When I was two or three, I was playing in the communal playground in Gardiner Street and fell off the third step on the stairway of an old steel slide. I managed to somehow fall directly on the back of my head and was struck unconscious. I was duly rushed to Temple Street Hospital and stayed there for a number of nights. I was unconscious for some hours, which must have been worrying for my mother and father, but in the middle of the night I woke up miraculously and called out for my parents. My father had stayed with me for my duration in hospital. It was during my convalescence that the doctors had to shave my head, for observation purposes, and this act, my mother asserts, is responsible for the change in my hair colour from brown to black and the alteration in its texture from straight to its current curley equivalent. The accident was something I would query later in life as the possible event that caused my chronic stuttering. However, it was only years later when I educated myself on the causal effects of stammering that I determined that stuttering is generally caused by genetic and environmental factors.

It quickly became apparent that Vicky's birth had generated all sorts of financial and housing problems for my young parents. The space in Gardiner Street was limited and my mother applied to be housed somewhere more suitable for a family with two children under the age of two.

Dublin Corporation duly acquiesced and my parents gathered their belongings and unsuspecting children and made the three-minute journey up the road to the newly built apartment complex of Mountain View Court in Summerhill.

In fairness, on a clear day, you *could* see the mountains, with a pair of binoculars. Although the design and layout of the apartments were rudimentary, our new place was opulent in comparison to Gardiner Street. My mother was especially pleased as she now had her parents and two sisters living in the same complex, providing much-needed childcare services and moral support when things got difficult between herself and my father.

My early memories of Mountain View Court were of gangs of children playing frantic football matches on newly built concrete pitches and the sound of traffic passing under my window every night as I tried to sleep. Later, as the children transformed into restless teenagers, the area became increasingly beset with crime. Drugs and joyriding decimated many such Corporation flats in the early 1980s and a high percentage of the children I had played alongside subsequently spent time in prison or became addicted to heroin.

Every summer there were community games held, which seemed to have been run by designated responsible residents with the assistance of Dublin Corporation. There were running and sprinting competitions, soccer competitions in Fairview Park and on the concrete soccer pitch at the very front of Mountain View Court that was adjacent to a car park (which always remained empty as no residents had any cars at that time). I received my first trophies and medals following my early victories in these competitions, often against oversized opponents who flagrantly ignored the age criteria for competing. The amenities were basic when we first moved in but later, as if my magic, a wooden maze that children could walk through appeared in the corner of a common area, painted in gaudy primary colours. The successful negotiation of the maze was not all that difficult, a sentiment eventually shared by the residents of the flats, and the maze was duly burnt one night by bored teenagers.

Sometimes, parents would compete in these soccer matches too and I vividly recall seeing my father leap in the air and perform a bicycle kick, sending the ball to the top corner of the goal (needless to say, Dublin Corporation did not provide nets).

My maternal grandparents lived two storeys above us in the same apartment complex and there were many times I dropped in with either my father or mother. I was always presented with sweet tea and chocolate biscuits. My grandfather, James, had worked all his life as a seaman with Irish Shipping, often spending months away from home on extended sea voyages. He boxed in his youth and his brother Spike McCormack was a renowned Irish boxing champion. Many years later I would read in Bill Cullen's autobiography of his recollection of a bare-knuckled boxing match between Spike and a local challenger outside the Sunset House pub in Summerhill. Spike triumphed after an epic encounter that left both competitors badly injured and exhausted.

My grandfather was a thoroughly caring and genuine man and would sit me on his knee, enthralling me by removing his false teeth and gurning obscene faces, ignoring the criticisms of his wife, Katie. My grandmother was one of the typical strong women of that age, having spent her life rearing nine children. She was garrulous and infectious and lit up a room with her smile and good humour. She was pious and devout and religious images, iconography and statuettes adorned the walls and were scattered around the mantelpiece and sundry tables. As a young boy, sometimes these images scared me, especially an over-realistic depiction of the crucifixion. She attended Mass every Sunday morning at St Lourdes Chapel in Seán McDermott Street in her blue overcoat and paisley headscarf that she wore outside irrespective of the climate or temperature.

It was while I was playing outside with the children who lived in the flats that I first began to notice how other people reacted to the way I spoke. I must have displayed signs of stammering with my family but it was obvious they felt that the matter should not be addressed and that hopefully over time my obvious speech blocks and struggles would disappear (a physical speech block happens when you are trying to push air out over your vocal chords to generate a sound but your body is too racked with fear and tension to raise the rib cage to generate the desired air flow. Your mouth is open but nothing is coming out). The other children, however, were not so compassionate. I was aware of being pointed at and being told by them that I talked funny or I made certain faces when I tried to enunciate certain words or sounds. I remember feeling frustrated many times by apparently not being physically able to convey what was going on in my mind at the time but I had no knowledge about what was happening with my speaking process. I obviously must have managed to relegate those uneasy thoughts to the back of my mind because I don't recall stammering ever being a huge issue in my life until I began primary school.

I do have memories of being in St Lawrence O'Toole's School before moving to O'Connell CBS; one vivid recollection I have is seeing a nun strike a child with a metre-long ruler, covered in red insulating tape, across his backside. The insulating tape must have been for dramatic effect. Perhaps it was my diminutive stature or my erroneous sense of proportion but that nun appeared to me to be taller than my father and as physically intimidating. I certainly don't remember anything enjoyable about my initial school experience. I know we had subsidised milk in real glass bottles every day for lunch and sometimes the luxury of ham and cheese sandwiches, though my stomach used to turn with the smell of the warm milk. Perhaps my mother's overzealousness as a young baby in gorging me with milk eventually took its toll on me.

My younger sister Emma arrived in 1981, without undue influence on me. I was oblivious to what my parents were going through at that time. I know there must have been money issues and my father was under pressure as the sole breadwinner. There definitely were times when the marriage was under pressure. At some point my mother left my father for a brief period and stayed with her mother. I have memories of seeing him struggling with the washing machine and me wondering where my mother was. It was a portent of things to come. My world revolved around being outside and kicking a ball around; it was irrelevant to me whether I was on my own or had someone to play with. My parents had also furnished me with an impressive array of toys over my short number of years. When the weather was warm, I played out on the balcony at the front of the flat, on a blanket put down by my mother, trying to avoid the drying sheets, clothes and bed linen that had been hung out to dry. I had all manner of cars and helicopters, Superman and other superhero action figures. I even had an outrageously inaccurate Superman costume complete with a plastic red cape that clipped together rather precariously around my neck. I lived in that costume for days on end.

Before primary school I was blissfully unaware of the difficulties that would be presented to me due to my stammer. I was also not aware of the prevailing atmosphere in the house and the strained relationship between my father and mother. The next few years would bring experiences and emotions that I would struggle with for the rest of my life.

2

Primary School Years

It was only when I started O'Connell CBS primary school and began to interact with other students and teachers that I suddenly realised speaking was going to become a huge obstacle in my life. My previous instances of speaking poorly with friends and family, once innocently put down as normal blips in my natural speech development, were quickly recalibrated as signs of a serious problem. There were changes at home too. I became increasingly aware of my father's mood swings and temper and how I was often the target of his fury.

When I started primary school my self-awareness and ability to detect tension in the house grew to almost superhuman levels. As well as discovering what a stammer actually was and how it was going to affect me, I also discovered flaws in my father and his character traits that I did not like. The deterioration in our relationship coincided with the development of my chronic childhood stammering.

We never had much money but my parents were always there; they never smoked or drank their money, and they fed us. My father had a savage work ethic and a determination to succeed and for us to better ourselves. He would always stand over me while I was doing homework and would order me to re-do sections that were not neat enough or did not meet a paternally imposed quality control criteria.

I developed that work ethic myself and believed from an early age that in order to have a better life, a more comfortable life, and to live anywhere except Corporation flats, I had to be good at school and education was the key. I was not a child musical prodigy, I was not going to marry a rich spinster and I was never going to be plucked from obscurity by some mystical power and be given a life of luxury. Unfortunately, I would have to work hard for it.

That manifested itself as early as eight or nine years old when I would get up at 5 o'clock in the morning and study until 6.30 a.m. every weekday. It made perfect sense to me. I could comfortably revise in the warmth of my bed the previous day's homework and lessons and be well prepared for the forthcoming school day. I also had to keep up my unspoken agreements with my teachers I had made in my own head (and which they had no knowledge of). I would do my best and be good at school, even at the subjects I did not like, if you Mr Teacher never asked me any questions in class or indeed make me verbalise any part of the school syllabus out loud to the class or to you personally, under any circumstances.

I found I had good memory retention and picked things up quickly and so I rather enjoyed doing this for a few years. In any event the weekday began at 5.00 a.m. and studying finished at 6.30 a.m. My father was also an early riser and would invariably rise at 6 to get himself ready for work (when available) and to start the day. In all the time I've known him I have never seen him lay in bed past 7.00 a.m. When he got up in the morning he always listened to the radio and then at 6.30 a.m he would turn on BBC 1. For some reason BBC 1 showed a twenty-minute 1940s American TV show called *Edgar Kennedy* every weekday morning for most of my childhood years. I watched it every day as my father toodled around in the kitchen making himself something to eat and preparing my breakfast. My breakfast was always two hard-boiled eggs, two pieces of toast and a mug of sweet tea.

I would sit on the armchair, my legs dangling over the end, in my pyjamas and dressing gown, the warm plate on my lap, enjoying Mr Kennedy's antics. Edgar was a rotund American (naturally), balding, middle-aged man, very much Homer Simpson-esque but without the quality scriptwriters *The Simpsons* had. He was a mixture of the Three Stooges, Laurel and Hardy, and Buster Keaton. Anyway, for twenty minutes he would try to remain calm while his wife and her extended family landed him in some comical situation or other at his own expense while he tried not to explode in the face of over-whelmingly annoying and vacuous individuals.

This programme always made me laugh and is one of the strongest positive memories I have associated with my father. In that hushed living room, in the darkness with only the black-and-white TV programme illuminating the room, I felt especially close to my father. Sometimes he would ask what Edgar was up to and I would stammer an answer about him being in trouble again, which technically he was, and then he would continue his morning ritual of tidying up and getting ready for the day ahead. By 7 a.m. my sisters and mother would begin their ritual of hair-brushing and dressing and eating, sometimes simultaneously but always tension-filled. Sure, you could not go to school without tension. Someone would say something that would ignite my father and that was that. In any event, my father had the ability to spontaneously ignite and really you had to see it to truly appreciate it. It was fairly shitty to be in the middle of it alright but well ... he certainly didn't do anything in half-measures. I remember having hugely conflicting emotions about my father at the time, hating the atmosphere in the house when there was a row while simultaneously grudgingly admiring the individual doing his best so that his children could achieve their full potential.

My mother told me that my father used to drink a lot up until I was two or three years old. So it seems my birth was not the catalyst for his sobriety but, according to her, the money was tight with the new baby and all (me) and therefore he decided simply to give up.

My father was an old-school disciplinarian and believed a clip around the ear was the answer to many parental problems. This was frequently accompanied by blazing rows and for as long as I remember he held a unique ability to make me cry. Once I had reached the point of pure despair and anguish and had been reduced to an emotional wreck the tears would flow and a pressure valve would seem to be released in my father. We would be best pals then and he would be sorry for having taken things so far. But, according to him, it was not his fault as there was no guide to parenthood he could read and no one ever tutored him on how to act as a father.

My father is a man of many contrasts and capable of vast extremes. I remember him having to sell his coat one Christmas to generate some funds for the family and I fondly recall listening carefully to his vast eclectic knowledge of 1960s British pop, the two world wars, the British Empire and any other facts he acquired and retained along the way. He was a keen reader, verbose, gregarious and street-wise, but lacked the encouragement or application that academic achievement requires. He left school at an early age and made his way to London in the late 1960s to try his luck. In his prime he was an imposing figure with a booming voice and matching personality, capable, assured and sometimes bombastic.

He is a desperate hard worker and remarkably self-disciplined. He was able to stop drinking overnight and later he became vegetarian in a similarly abrupt manner. He loves being alone, being outside in rustic conditions and particularly sea fishing. He loves sport (though he could never seem to get his head around hurling) and lived his dreams vicariously through his children.

One thing that always stayed with me was how, in many of his anger-filled emotional outbursts, he would purposefully hit his head against the wall a couple of times to express his frustration at how invariably I – and sometimes my sisters – behaved. He would explain later on that this was for our benefit; how else could he show how much we annoyed him? Perhaps he could have just said to us how frustrated he felt. Like any normal human being.

But that's the type of man he is; he certainly does not do half-measures. Watching someone bang their head off a wall may have some comic quality, but when you are a child and everyone around you is shrieking in terror there is no comedy involved. This kind of behaviour persisted and incrementally worsened to such an extent that the episodes were almost daily. In order to avoid them, I would walk for hours around the city centre with a Sony Walkman tucked inside my jacket, listening to music, until such time as it was bedtime or night-time or match time or school time or whatever it was that had to be done. I would stay out of the firing line before something else kicked my father off.

Music was a huge escape and solace. The early albums of REM with their jangly guitars and incomprehensible lyrics were restructured in my brain so that they only applied to me and my situation.

I was amazed about how much Michael Stipe knew about my predicament but I was glad he did. Every other group at that time seemed to be singing about love, lost love, unrequited love or wanting to be loved. It would be a few more years before I would be interested in that sort of thing.

A constant and intractable issue that dominated home life was my stammer and my increasing inability to control my speech – and the realisation that there was nothing I could do to help myself.

The stammer was just really bad luck on my behalf. It is hereditary, from my mother's side, but coupled with parental ignorance, my shyness, my over-sensitivity to the world around me and the problems at home it was never tackled at the right time and became progressively worse as I grew up. A good majority of children stammer as they learn the communication process and most grow out of it but I didn't and that's that. Most children have trouble striking a sliotar with a hurl out of the hand but I didn't; the gods certainly were capricious.

So I became locked into a vicious cycle of my sensitivity, shyness and stammer constantly annoying my father, inadvertently, who would ignite. And these associated negative feelings lay buried inside me because I could not deal with them or even verbalise them to anyone. All the while my frustration at myself, and my resentment towards my father, grew.

The feelings became powerful and manifested themselves as suicidal thoughts. I was overwhelmed with these feelings caused by the stress and anxiety at home while struggling with the normal teenage years, burgeoning hormones and deciding who I really was, what I like and what man I was going to become. The one word I would use to describe this period is *tense*. I believe that the mental health problems I faced in my late thirties stem principally from my inability to personally deal with the situation at home, my stammer and my perception of how redundant I was at verbal communication.

My stammer is a physical manifestation of a neurological disorder. The struggles, blocks, word and sound repetitions, filler words and long silent pauses that you see when I speak are only 10 per cent of the disorder that has affected every single second of my life for nearly 30 years.

Recent research indicates that the pathway from the creation of speech thoughts in the brain is hindered somewhere along the process to actual speech production. Individually the parts of the system work but collectively they are mostly out of sync.

I have my own theory in that genetically I have always had the predisposition to stammer. Stammering runs in my mother's family and we have certain common characteristics that create a potential stammering host: we do not deal with stress easily, we suffer anxiety, we worry, we take things to heart, we think about things too much, we bury our feelings and we do not like confrontation. But I also feel that some environmental factors growing up triggered the stammering behaviour. That is my personal opinion and I know that many of the stammerers I have met along my journey feel the same way. I would love to be able to pinpoint an exact occasion when I acknowledged the presence of my stammering. I could therefore endeavour to deal with the emotional impact of that event to try to deal with my current stammering behaviour. However, it was never going to be that easy.

I stammered from the time I began to learn to speak.

I stammered all the time and sometimes when there was tension in the household my stammering would be more pronounced than normal. I quickly noticed a direct correlation between the atmosphere in the home and my speaking performance.

It was always the elephant in the room. No one in the family openly talked about or acknowledged my stammer but its presence was palpable. There was never a situation where I would initiate a conversation with my parents because I simply could not physically sustain one. I think my parents knew I was extremely uncomfortable about stammering, even the word 'stammer' or 'stutter' was never used. I hated the word; I hated the sound it made when people said it. I hated every time I heard it or read it.

I therefore had these environmental factors impacting on my genetic tendencies, all leading to the creation and perpetuation of stammering.

At some point my mother decided that an intervention was required. One of my earliest memories from this time is of my mother and I on our visits to the Speech and Language Department of Temple Street Hospital in Dublin. There is an archway over the entrance to a tunnel leading to the hospital from Mountjoy Square. I distinctly remember holding my mother's hand and looking up at her as we walked toward the hospital every week. I know there was a therapist there with red hair, Mrs Sweeney, and there was a green plastic sandpit with some old toy cars to play with. I have some recollection of talking to Mrs Sweeney and sitting in a big black leather chair with my legs swinging under me. I don't know what we talked about but I know I felt a certain acceptance but I also felt different because not all boys of my age were going there.

I also remember the waiting room was always crowded and I know there was another boy there named Ronan, because his mother always used to call his name. He must have been misbehaving every week. I know this is strange but I also thought the whole process was an absolute waste of time. I can't have been more than six at the time but I definitely felt a total sense of hopelessness in Temple Street. I also had a feeling that my mother wanted something 'big' to happen. She would always look at me expectantly on the way home but I couldn't figure out why at the time.

Then all of a sudden, it seemed, we stopped going; I don't know why. I think I felt some relief about not having to go but I don't recall a specific reason why the sessions ended and I certainly don't remember feeling any incremental improvement in my mood as a result of the visits. In fact my moods darkened as my playmates continuously focused on my speech and blocks. I began to play on my own and avoid other children. I associated playing with others with being jeered or ridiculed. This is when my avoidance behaviours began in earnest.

My first specific school stammering memory is in second class in primary school, which would make me seven or eight. I remember the teacher threatened me with reading aloud if I spoke to a classmate again while his back was turned. I remember instantly feeling two things – fear of having to deal with the punishment but an even greater sense of shame and embarrassment that everyone therefore must know I have difficulty speaking in class if this was the unique punishment offered to me. Already, as early as second class in primary school, I was building up huge emotional baggage surrounding my speech and my own speaking process.

Primary school continued generally in the same vein. I am prin-cipally an overt stammerer. This means it is obvious when I begin the speaking process that I stammer – from the facial expressions, the bouncing on sounds and words, the lack of breath, the lack of eye contact, and the body movements and jerking. However, I would also scan words in advance for feared words or sounds. I would try to word substitute or to re-arrange the pattern of words so that I would at least have reduced difficulty saying words that I knew I could verbalise a little better. I would also pretend to not know the answers to questions and in extreme cases, like when asked my name, respond with another name beginning with a word or sound that I was not have difficulty with at the time. These are classic behaviours of a covert stammerer.

I attended O'Connell Schools CBS primary school on North Richmond Street. My first teachers certainly did not make me feel comfortable with myself or my stammer in school. I know that my mother had to speak with certain teachers a few times to explain about my general shyness and disability which manifested itself whenever I opened my mouth. I remember in third class there were two other boys in my class with stammers, which statistically was very unusual. The general consensus is that about 1 per cent of the population is affected by stammering so having three pupils in the same class with a stammer was rare, or more specifically unfortu-nate for all concerned. Although statistically challenged with three stammerers in his class, the teacher ploughed on and he adopted the approach that everyone in the class would participate and read aloud, irrespective of disability. I remember dreading going to school knowing I would have to endure sniggers and lingering sideways looks when I stumbled over passages I would have to read. In those days I don't think there was any specific training or guidance for teachers. Certainly their treatment and attitude towards me and my stammer varied throughout primary school and indeed bordered on sadism in secondary school. In truth, I was embarrassed for myself and embarrassed for the other two guys when they stuttered in class. I knew *exactly* how they felt when they started to blush before reading. Sometimes my legs would tremble under the desk before I spoke while another guy would have to thump his leg rhythmi-cally to try to get his words out. We each had our different coping mechanisms. We were just some innocent kids trying to come to terms with this ... fucking thing ... inside us that made us different from everyone else and made you feel like shit because you couldn't express how you felt ... or say what the capital of Ireland was because D sounds always make you block. Even when you knew what the capital was, and what the capital of England was, and the capital of every country in Western Europe.

The misery I was experiencing speaking in school was countered by the joy I had playing sports. O'Connell's prioritised Gaelic football and hurling, and every day during lunch and after school we would be taught drills, like catching and kicking a football, catching and striking a sliotar, and developing these skills in furious matches where someone was always split open, patched together and the ball thrown in to continue. I found I had some natural ability in that I picked up new skills fast, I was quick and agile, but most of all I wanted to practice on my own and develop myself further. I saw football and hurling as my first real means of expressing myself and I wanted to be known as the fella who is really good at hurling as opposed to the fella in class who could not talk. I was also diminutive as a child and early teenager and preferred hurling over football at an early age because you could be very good at hurling despite your size disadvantage once you had a strong skillset. I liked this idea and practiced diligently.

The best part of my day was always lunch time when Mr O'Keeffe would wander into the yard with a bag of old hurleys and Gaelic footballs slung across his shoulder. Anyone who was interested could grab a hurley or football and position himself against the huge flat wall at the end of the yard and literally go nuts striking or kicking for the remainder of lunch. The hurleys were invariably always the wrong size, shape and weight but it didn't matter because there was always delight in striking a ball (we were not allowed sliotars in the yard, only tennis balls) against the wall. The really good guys could actually catch the ball on the way back from the wall. I remember thinking to myself, as I frantically scurried after ball after ball that I failed to catch, that I would never be able to master this skill.

If you played on the school team you could have the pick of the hurleys from the bag but sometimes, every so often, you could be lucky and be mysteriously left with a hurley exactly matching your specifications. Your chances of successfully striking and catching a ball rose substantially if you had the right hurley.

Mr O'Keeffe would inspect your progress as you toiled against the wall, interjecting with succinct comments about shortening your grip, widening your stance and other pearls of wisdom. If you struck the ball cleanly or controlled it you would always look over your shoulder to see if Mr O'Keeffe was watching and await his approving nod.

When I was eleven I was selected to play for a combined Dublin schools' football team which were to play an exhibition game in Casement Park in Belfast. I don't know if it was necessarily the most skilful kids who went (judging by our performance) but it was a great achievement nonetheless to wear the Dublin jersey at any level. There was some trepidation in my family because it was at the height of the Troubles in the North and at a time when walking around Belfast with a hurley or Gaelic football in your hand could bring unfortunate consequences. In any event, we all gathered at the coach and waved our goodbyes. I was filled with excitement and was looking forward to playing in a fine stadium liked Casement Park, which would regularly host matches for the Antrim county teams as well as Ulster football and hurling finals.

I was also acutely aware that I did not know anyone else on the team or any of the management and that somewhere along the journey my stutter would be revealed and that would be the end of my enjoyment. I started the journey in hope but it wasn't long before everyone was introducing themselves and sharing details of their clubs, schools and positions played. As expected, all eyes turned to me as I struggled with my name and the incredulous looks and giggling continued for the length of the journey. As bonds were forming and the spirits rose the jokes began and the boy in the seat directly in front of mine stood up and told a joke about a stuttering boy and how he had to rhyme a song in order to complete a sentence. The joke was spectacularly uninventive but elicited the desired response of stifled laughter and various sideways looks towards me as I sunk deeper into my seat, blushing profusely. I buried myself under my coat for the remainder of the journey, pretending to sleep while inwardly trying to rationalise the behaviour of the comedian. I couldn't understand that level of insensitivity, even at that tender age, toward someone you did not know and, worse, was part of your team.

The rest of the day was a blur and I held back tears as we departed from the bus, entered the impressive dressing rooms and pulled on our oversized Dublin jerseys. I rolled up my sleeves, tucked the excess fabric of my jersey into my shorts and promised myself that I would show everyone who laughed at me on the bus what a great player I was. Despite my desperate attempts to play well, I only got a few minutes playing time (it was only fair that everyone partic-ipated) but every minute I was out on the pitch I was thinking of smashing the comedian's face in. I was so filled with hatred (towards him and myself for not having an acerbic witty retort) that I let the day slip past me when I should have been enjoying every minute of it.

We received our shiny medals, ate a meal of bacon and cabbage, and settled down in the coach for the journey home. I just couldn't grasp the necessity for that joke. My sensitivity had gone into hyper-drive and ruined my day. I kept roleplaying in my head different scenarios where I would laugh at the joke myself, respond with an expletive-filled threat, break the comedian's nose or launch a similar diatribe at him, mocking the length of his nose and his dismal skin complexion. I kept thinking to myself, how the fuck do I stop this from happening again?

Things got a little bit more serious in sixth class as we prepared for secondary school. I was going to attend O'Connell Schools CBS secondary school, which shared the same yard and grounds as the primary school. I liked the sixth class teacher, Mr Courtney. He was encouraging and enthusiastic and he later became a fine principal of the school.

I was studious and diligent. I fundamentally liked to learn new things. I was not a fan of homework as it took time away from playing sport after school, but I grudgingly did it to the best of my ability because my family constantly reinforced in us the belief that you had to do well in school in order to succeed in life. There was some parental pressure but I put enough pressure on myself to keep motivated and I achieved good grades throughout primary school.

Mr Courtney appeared to be empathetic toward my speech issues and encouraged me to participate more in class than my previous teachers. He organised a year-long competition amongst the class where groups of students working together as a team competed against other groups for a token trophy and the glory of being the 'super team' for that year. I was made captain of one of those teams. Mr Courtney christened us Benham's Bandits. Each group was awarded points for the quality of homework and projects completed but also, much more importantly, points were awarded for achievement in sport, PE and specialised football matches that would occur in the yard and sometimes Fairview Park. It was a great way to motivate students and everyone willingly rowed in.

Every day in PE and the organised matches fellas would kill themselves trying to win just to grab the coveted points for their teams. Mr Courtney would also review everyone's homework every afternoon. You would approach his desk, patiently wait as he scanned the material and receive your marks out of ten for your hard work. The points were added up and then accumulated over the days and weeks until finally, a month before the end of the school year, the trophy was awarded to ... Benham's Bandits! We had earned bragging rights for the rest of the school year.

Mr Courtney organised a class play for the end of the year and, despite my attempts to get out of it, I was cast in the role of a farmer's wife. The plot eludes me now but I remember having to say a few lines, push the story forward and hand things over to the rest of the guys. I was terrified. I blocked whenever I tried the lines in my own speaking voice but one day I tried to say the words in a country accent and the words flowed effortlessly. I realised I had stumbled onto a very valuable tool and was determined to use it. When the time came for me to act my lines I spoke fluently (albeit with a very dubious country accent). At the time I did not know why there was a marked difference in the quality of my speech due to the adoption of a different persona. It was only nearly twenty years later, on the McGuire Programme, that I understood why my speech flowed that day and I did not stutter. I was allowing myself to be someone else; I was speaking not from the grounded base of a chronic stammerer but as a world-weary country farmer's wife. I was also having fun with the role, expressing myself, letting go of any inhibitions and my mind was not filled with pre-event anxiety or tension but with the effort of trying to master the voice.

As the school year wore on Mr Courtney would speak to me about secondary school. He knew the difficulties I was going to face but he wanted to reassure me that I could confront the speaking problems that secondary school was going to throw at me. Despite my thespian success I was realistic enough to appreciate the next year was going to be challenging (at best). I was going to have to deal with new people, new teachers, new structures and once again I was going to have to go through the excruciating process of revealing my stutter to strangers.

During the summer before secondary school I withdrew deeper into myself as I imagined the impending embarrassment and self-hate that awaited me. The tension in the household remained and I tried to remain out of my father's line of sight as much as possible.

Money was always an issue with my father and a constant source of concern and worry for him. He was unemployed at that time, which was tremendously stressful not just for him but for the rest of the family also. Every day he had to look at himself in the mirror and the burden of providing for the family inevitably affected his temperament.

My mother always tried her best to deflate the situation when a row erupted but her efforts were largely futile. She must have realised early on in her marriage what a difficult husband she had but after her initial brief separation from my father she settled into a difficult life with him for the sake of her children. She is physically diminutive but she diminished further when my father's temper flared. She has not got the skills to deal with his behaviour and the consequent conflict. When things started to get somewhat physical and my father slapped me about the head she would try to protect me, yelling at my father to calm down while pleading with me to stop crying. She tried her best. It perhaps was a generational thing to stick with the marriage despite it being ultimately self-destructive. My approach was simple: avoid being anywhere near my father. I took long walks; I went hurling; I stayed in my room; I read; I thought about my father and my family relationships; and I thought about my stammer. A lot.

The strange thing was I desperately wanted a relationship with my father. I wanted stability. I wanted to have the same father every day when I walked in from school. I did not want the fractious figure who dominated the house. I wanted to show him what I could do with a hurl and ball. I wanted to talk to him about my troubles in school and about the way I talked. I *needed* to talk to him about my life. It was so frustrating to want to have this connection with my father but every argument cumulatively destroyed these sentiments.

When I was younger he would take me sea-fishing, digging bait and with long walks to that desired spot where the chances of catching fish were maximised. I enjoyed these moments. He was always happiest out of the house, away from the problems that enveloped our little flat, doing some physical activity. We would take the first early-morning DART to Killiney or Greystones. We would proudly carry our fishing gear and talk excitedly about how many we would catch today. Sometimes we would get off one or two stations before the final destination and walk the rest, enjoying the sea air and sunrise. My father would argue that soccer is more manly and entertaining than hurling while I shook my head and outlined the case for the defence.

We would set up our rods and rests on the stony beach, erect a little camp and I'd wait as my father readied the rods, put bait on the hooks and cast both rods into the sea. Once the tautness of the lines was just right, he would settle down, open a flask of tea and spend the next few hours watching the top of the rod as it bobbed and waivered with the movement of the sea. Every so often there would be a noticeable bend in the rod as unsuspecting fish nibbled and gnawed on the bait and my father would leap up, grab the rod, secure it between his legs and slowly reel in what was tugging on the line. Invariably it was nothing but every time he leaped up I hoped it was a fish so that we could proudly present it to my mother for filleting later that evening.

But my memories always returned to what he had said at the last argument, the way he had destroyed my confidence and made me cry. At the time, the stuff he said was soul-destroying but nearly thirty years later I understand what was happening to him. It was only after having children myself that I realised how difficult parenting is. I was immersed in my own world of self-doubt, negativity and pity, and I learned from an early age not to engage with my father. That frustrated him and I knew it then but I was not compelled to do anything about it. We all carried on regardless and things just got worse.

I was worried about secondary school. I was worried about everything. I remember I used to go to the car park in Mountain View Court and hurl a ball off the wall for hours on end. Usually I would go early in the morning when there was no one around and less chance of someone approaching and asking me for 'a shot of the hurley stick'. I was there to practice and to get better before trying out for the school teams in secondary school. I remember one afternoon my mother and I went shopping and she bought me a brand-new hurley and real leather sliotar in Clery's. It was the first brand new hurley I ever owned and I treasured it. I wore the leather off the sliotar on the first day from striking it against the concrete wall and practiced a variety of skills I would need to be selected for the future school team: sideline cuts, frees, lifting and striking without handling the ball, doubling in the air. I devoured the hurling matches that were shown on TV and memorised how certain players moved, positioned themselves, read the play and carried themselves even when the ball was nowhere near them. I was educating myself without even knowing it.

I was also becoming much more aware of the changes in my body before, during and after speaking. For a long time, my stutter was just there, like a weight I carried across my shoulders that revealed itself immediately when I spoke. But I began to anticipate speaking situations and develop severe self-hatred about my inability to communicate. I did not have any tools or techniques to deal with the physical components of stuttering nor the associated psychological issues that came with repeated speech blocks. I was developing avoidance behaviours, anxiety, self-hate, self-guilt, shame and embarrassment.

I had to blame somebody, someone, for giving me this affliction. I, probably unjustly, blamed my father at some level for my stammer but someone else ignored my nightly pleas to be able to talk fluently in the morning. God. Yeah, he became the ultimate fall guy. I suppose that is where my scepticism about religion started. I could not understand why I was selected to have this thing inside me when I was intrinsically a good person. I was having enough issues at home without the additional burden of stuttering. I would look at the situation logically and conclude it was simply unfair. If some higher power had determined that I deserved a lifetime of stuttering then fuck *him*. If I had that power then it would be more judicially implemented. There were at least a dozen kids I'd known from the flats who definitely deserved a life of stuttering, self-hate and embarrassment. Not me. I was a good kid. I was just interested in school work, hurling and football.

The trouble with being in a Christian Brother school was the emphasis given to religion and especially the quantity of preparatory work needed to be performed by pupils before they were confirmed. The work involved getting to know the Holy Spirit, the sacrament of Confession, the Body of Christ and other terms that have been indoctrinated into children for so many years. We had many fresh-faced and innocent priests come to our class and preach to us what a wonderful event Confirmation was going to be in our lives. They all looked the same and coincidentally always wore the same type of thick-soled black shoes. I surmised they did a lot of walking. They all spoke from the same script and seemed genuinely excited about what they were talking about. I could appreciate that; man, I would love to spend the day talking about hurling if I did not stutter.

I don't know why but I never fully comprehended the necessity for this religious fervour. It just wasn't for me. Stammering had begun to harden me somewhat. I had endured a few emotional knocks along the way. I didn't have the inclination to draw pictures showing Jesus loving me when he ignored me every night. Everybody seemed to believe in this ... religious movement, but I would shake my head incredulously. However, my desire to be a diligent pupil countered my latent atheism and I undertook all necessary work in order to stand with my fellow classmates in our leather jackets and hideous 1980s suits as the bishop waved his incense and did whatever he did to complete our Confirmations.

Part of my scepticism came from my father. He had a mistrust of all things ecclesiastical and often said that becoming a priest was taking the easy way out of life. Sure, they wouldn't have to find a job, work for a living, raise kids or pay bills. I kind of saw his point. I remember the local priest coming to visit the flat one day. He was new to the community and eager to connect with the lost sheep in his flock. My mother had let him into the house while my father was out but on his return he tutored the young priest on why he had chosen the wrong path in life, outlined the futility of his work, returned the envelope the priest had given my mother for 'church dues' and assured the priest that if any of his family wanted religious guidance they would seek it from the Protestant church in town. The priest never called around again.

To emphasise the point my father once told me a story about his own father in Kent. Every year to celebrate the local harvest, various members of the community would place baskets of fruit, vegetables and other produce they had grown and cultivated on the altar of the local church under the watchful gaze of the elderly parish vicar. Everyone participated and the altar quickly filled up with the wonderful bounty. When all the respected members of the community had delivered their produce that they had slaved over for a year, in walked my grandfather. He confidently walked up the church aisle, holding a singular can of Heinz baked beans, placed it on the altar and, satisfied with his contribution, exited the church to admonishing looks and open mouths.

I would have liked to have known that man.

I also remember being terrified of going to confession, partly because of my stammer but also because I was going into a darkened secluded space with an unknown adult male, with halitosis, who was going to discuss all the bad things I had done in my life up to that point. Even at twelve I knew something was definitely not right about this whole thing. About believing in what you cannot see, about committing yourself to something with no tangible benefits.

Most of all I was angry with God. He could absolve me from all stammering in an instant and my life would be transformed into a magical and enjoyable experience. But he didn't. He left me to block when talking to people. He let them mock me. He stood aside as they made jokes on crowded coaches and ruined days like the trip to Belfast for me.

I withdrew further into myself, from my family and tried to formulate a way that I could just get by for the next few years. I was not very successful.

3

Secondary School

My summer of hurling against the wall and of quiet introspection came to an abrupt end. My parents and I had to attend a semi-interview with the principal of the secondary school with a view to sizing me up and making sure everyone knew about school policy, expectations and repercussions if protocols were breached. The principal was an imposing, balding, overweight and stern Christian Brother who tried to be welcoming and empathetic to the problems of raising children, despite knowing absolutely nothing about it. What was obvious was that he was passionate about education and providing the children in the school with every advantage he could offer in order for them to succeed academically. He was interested in my father's background, secretly appalled at his religion, pleased with my mother's and spoke proudly about the academic achievements of the school and the successes on the sports pitches. My ears pricked up. He wanted all new pupils to participate as much as they could in the extracurricular activities. He enquired whether I was interested in joining one of the debating teams. Just to say I had not opened my mouth in the interview up to this point so when my parents looked at each other knowingly during the awkward silence that followed, he quickly moved on to the school hurling and football teams.

I stammered a line about being interested in playing for the school teams. He nodded his head in approval and, ignoring my interrupted speech, encouraged me to try out for the teams when the term began. He was aware of my general grades from the primary school, briefly commented on my performance in Maths, Irish and English (good, but always room for improvement) and promised me that I would thoroughly enjoy my secondary school years.

I was fortunate in that there were a good number of guys from my sixth class in primary school returning as nervous first years in secondary school. At least they knew about my stutter. The problem would be the other pupils in the class who were unknown to me and how they would react when they were introduced to my stammer.

I was never specifically bullied in primary school over my speech. I was confident and assured playing sports and somehow that confidence, though very much distilled, remained with me in the yard. My fellow pupils, apart from the odd giggle and sly comment, were mostly gracious in their acceptance and understanding of my speech issues when reading in class. What also helped was my ability at sports and my academic performance. I don't feel I was ever considered a target or vulnerable enough for intimidation like other children may have been in school. I put myself through my own emotional torture. The difficulty was always meeting new people who did not know me and who viewed my stammer as an opportunity to ridicule and diminish me without getting to know me. I had come through this process in primary school, meeting new people, sharing experiences and revealing my stammer to them and gradually earning their respect and – perhaps friendship is too strong a word, but – their acceptance. I was known as, yes, the guy who stuttered but *also* the guy on the school team, the guy who played hurling in the yard all through lunch and the guy to talk to if you have problems with your Maths homework. I was dreading having to go through this process again in secondary school.

The additional fly in the ointment was that in secondary school there was a different teacher for every subject and therefore I had to build a rapport and working relationship with nine or ten separate teachers, with different personalities, different teaching methods and probably different attitudes towards stammering and dealing with a student of theirs who stammered.

One of the very earliest classes we had in secondary school was French. At this stage I did not know all of my classmates and seated myself within the confines of the students who were with me in primary school. The French teacher introduced himself and immediately went around the class, asking everyone to count sequentially in French after he had prompted you with the French version. I was sitting at the right side of the class, near the back and from the moment the first student (sitting on the left-hand side near the blackboard) began reciting, my body exploded with adrenaline. I was only just beginning to understand what my body went through during this pre-event anxiety but as it became closer to my time to speak my breathing became more erratic and my heart rate rocketed. When it was my turn to speak the students who knew me turned away and looked downward while the new students looked in my direction, seeking an explanation for the long pause. My mouth was open but no air was flowing out of my lungs over my vocal chords. I was in the middle of a huge block. I eventually choked out some sound. There was another long pause. After what seemed like an eternity the teacher nodded to the student sitting immediately behind me to continue.

As the remaining students continued trying their luck articulating numbers in French, I sank further down into my desk. The teacher stood at the top of a class and queried, 'Mr Benham, have you a problem with a stutter?' It did not take a master of deductive reasoning to know I was a stutterer but I did not appreciate the question in the middle of the class, half of whom did not know me. I wanted to stand up and shout, 'Yes I have but it doesn't fucking matter. Have you a problem putting the ball over the bar from 60 yards?' But I didn't. I lifted my head just long enough to nod and the class resumed. I was blushing profusely as I felt the new students' eyes burn holes in me. At least they know now, I said to myself.

Once again, my sensitivity ran riot and I imagined everyone spending the lunch break talking about me and finding ways to further humiliate me. The familiar self-hate and self-guilt followed. I pitied myself. I felt betrayed by God. I hated God. I hated my French teacher. I hated school. I hated stammering and I hated myself. I spent the rest of that day reliving the experience in my mind but despite replaying it a million times over there was never any occurrence where I had spoken confidently, without stuttering. That was totally out of the realms of possibility. My mind was utterly convinced that every time I opened my mouth in school I would block. This was my mindset during my first day in secondary school.

Looking back, the teacher should have spoken to me personally about my stammer. He didn't and that was that. I don't know if it was ignorance or lack of empathy on his part. Ideally, he should have known about me before the class started but there was no use thinking such thoughts at the time. I thought about whether it was a deliberate attempt to embarrass me and maybe break me down before the school year began. When I think back on these events as an adult I have very mixed feelings. I wanted to be treated differently and I wanted teachers to have to adjust their teaching style so that I could endure their class without my legs trembling in terror on the off-chance they would ask me a question. I'm sure other pupils with learning difficulties or reading difficulties were accommodated and at that time I wanted similar concessions for me.

Those thoughts appear selfish and defeatist to me now. I should have been focused on trying to improve my speech. Speech therapy or any other forms of rehabilitation never even entered my mind as being necessary during school. My reasoning was that it was tried in the past and didn't work. I held a deeply ingrained belief at a very early age that I was different because of the way I spoke. I definitely would have called it a disability, a handicap and something that I was going to have to battle with for the rest of my life. I just wanted a little compassion from the teachers. Perhaps I should have discussed it at length with them myself and made them aware of the terror I felt every day. But to me the very act of stammering revealed that terror. You could see it on my face, all the emotions I would go through before, during and after speaking. Why the fuck would you ask me a question when it *kills* me to answer it for you? Why would you put me through that MISERY? Surely you can tell I am SUFFERING here?

I thought about speaking to my parents about the school situation and possibly having them come to the school and talk to the year head teacher. I didn't. The continuing problems at home established an emotional chasm between us. When I came in from school I went to my room or went to the wall hurling until such time as I had to do my homework. I wanted to be alone with my own thoughts. When they asked, I told them that school was fine, that I was managing and that it was all ok. I just gritted my teeth and tried to get on with things as best I could.

Despite being revealed by my French teacher, I had to admit that he was a brilliant teacher, well-adjusted, practical and, if you carefully steered him in the right direction, he would spend the whole class talking about the current book he was reading or something that interested him while watching television the previous evening. He was very supportive all through secondary school to me and got me to grudgingly participate verbally in all his classes throughout the years; I reciprocated by consistently obtaining top marks in any vocabulary or reading comprehension tests he gave. I think my stammer intrigued him somewhat as some days, as my confidence ebbed and flowed, it would become more or less pronounced. He kept me on my toes and pushed me, which is a sign of a good teacher.

I noticed that some of the other teachers did not seek verbal contributions from students and in the majority of their classes they ended up doing all the work. During those classes, I could relax and enjoy the subject matter that was being taught to me. Some teachers were strict disciplinarians and would have no trouble screaming in your face if you stepped out of line. Once a few weeks passed everyone settled into the new regime, the students knew what infuriated the teachers and the teachers came to know the students who needed special additional supervision and correction.

However, there was one teacher who caused me problems. The Geography and History teacher would make us rote learn a passage every day. He would spend about half the subsequent class listening to every pupil recite, word for word, the previous day's passage. I was third to recite the passage by virtue of where my desk was positioned. For three years I had to endure this waiting, the foreboding and then the actual event itself. Every day I would be subjected to having to stand up and simply struggle to recite a piece that everybody could complete in or around two minutes. To this day I do not want to know what went on in that teacher's head when he saw me struggle every day with this. I don't understand people like that.

The stammering block is precipitated by minutes, hours, days and even years of pre-event anxiety. Extreme anxiety. There is such a pathological fear of stammering, of having a block, appearing foolish in front of others, appearing different, being laughed at, being ridiculed, that I can only compare it to instances where I thought I lost one of my children in the shopping centre. Your heart beats at a chest-destroying rate. You perspire heavily. Your stomach knots. Your clarity diminishes. Your thought processes are cloudy. And then you begin to speak. For me, on my worst days, my chest and breathing processes stop working and I cannot generate any air for the vocal chords to function. My blocks are mostly silent but prolonged. As I try to generate air over my vocal chords I choke the air out, resulting in spasms in my chest, neck and vocal chords. My mind is trying to regain some focus and control but my body is in self-preservation mode and wants to stop talking, to sit down and to relax. But I am forcing my whole system to undergo a process that has become habitual but supremely unnatural. If there is a problem or feared word or sound I try to generate sounds from unnatural movements in my head, neck, lips and tongue. I generate guttural, breathy sounds but nothing resembling normal speech. I cannot generate air. I get dizzy. My face goes red. I get headaches.

During a speech block I am supremely aware of my audience. I really care what they are thinking, where they are looking and what their reaction is. This affects my efforts at making coherent sounds. However, as my blocks continue my levels of anger and frustration grow and I am trapped in a continuous cycle of struggle. The only way I can avoid going through this experience again is by pretending I am a mute.

My fellow pupils would complete the learnt passage in about two minutes. I would frequently pass the 10-to-15-minute mark. Some days I would be told to sit down after only a couple of minutes struggling with the first word. Obviously the teacher's patience and empathy had a finite limit. I especially loathed it when I was forced to sit down without completing the passage. At least there was some dignity in completing the passage but not in being made to retire early. I know I struggled to look anyone in the eye for hours after such instructions.

I had the pleasure of looking forward to this experience every day for three school years.

As secondary school progressed, the patterns repeated themselves: the same cycle of pre-event anxiety, waiting to be called to
speak, failing miserably to speak and feeling the post-event shame,
guilt and self-hate. I had physical problems too arising from the
constant state of nervous tension I was in. I suffered from extreme
and frequent headaches, stomach problems and skin problems,
culminating in ulcers in later life. I had irregular sleep patterns and
would be prone to excessive mood swings. I had periods where my
moods were contrasting and would change instantly. One moment
I would be thinking about my future, about maybe one day playing
senior hurling for Dublin, feeling positive and excited, and then
another thought about a failed speaking occasion would jump into
my head and counteract my positive mood. I worried about my
future, about the many events and occasions at which I would have
to speak well in order for me to succeed in the game of life. I thought
about getting a job, getting married and having kids. I was worried
about dying alone, about not being able to control my speech enough
to hold down a job. I worried about not being successful and not
having the courage to endure the challenges in life that my stammer
presented. I was always worrying excessively, taking matters out
of context, reading too much into perceived slights, comments or
deemed failures and not blithely overcoming them the way everyone
else seemed to do with the regular setbacks they experience in life. It
would be almost twenty years until I would sit down with a psychologist and piece together the threads that would lead me to finding
some answers. Sometimes I would think about ending my life and
weigh quite objectively the pros and cons of surviving another week,
month or year. I tried to put a structure on my life experiences,
noting them down on paper and generating a form of equation. If
negative experiences and feelings are greater than the positive ones,
why continue living? I always felt I was not strong enough to deal
with the lifetime of stammering that I had predicted for myself.
There was never an occasion where I thought to myself that I would
eventually somehow grow out of stammering or obtain the tools and
techniques to control it. Sometimes, after an especially bad speaking
experience, for instance, if I responded to someone asking me my
name with a name that I could easily verbalise, like Mark or John, I
would subsequently punish myself for my cowardice. I would go and

run until I would almost collapse. I would abstain from eating until I would be weak with the hunger or go to the hurling wall and hit the ball until the strain on my wrists and forearms were so great that I could not grasp the hurley. That frustration and self-hatred would reduce me to a crying wreck.

My already shrunken belief in divine intervention did not prevent me from pleading for help from above. I had a prayer I would recite every night that evolved from 'God, please let the stammer go away in the morning' to a rather darker 'Please, please, do not let me wake up in the morning.' When I woke up in the morning I cursed God and braced myself for the impending battles ahead.

My stammering affected everything in my life. Despite retiring to my room immediately when I arrived home from school, my parents began to notice the introspective changes in my personality and my darkening moods. My family are typical Dublin working class and certainly could not afford private speech therapy for me. However, my father had read about the benefits of hypnotherapy and booked an initial consultation with a guy in town. I remember seeing my father hand over an envelope of money to this guy at the start and sitting in front of him at his desk as he gave me a newspaper to read aloud. I guess this was an assessment of both my reading ability and the degree of severity of my stammer. When that was completed he took me through a relaxation and meditation session and we began to read the newspapers aloud again. At this point my father entered the room and we continued with the reading. I remember my father saying to me, 'How are you, how do you feel ...?' I don't think I did too well. The hypnotherapy guy gave my father back his money in the same envelope.

From the time I was fifteen I was experiencing frequent headaches. These would invariably begin in the late afternoon and sometimes continue throughout the night. I put these down to the tension I was experiencing at home and the continued effort to force words out while stammering (which was effectively every time I spoke). I began to self-medicate with over-the-counter painkillers and from that time I also carried a box of painkillers everywhere I went. The headaches occurred regularly, at least four times a week. It did not occur to me to discuss the situation with my parents and indeed I never understood the potential consequences of self-medicating.

I would continue to take over-the-counter painkillers all through my teenage years. Before I became proficient in my use of them I would have to crush them up and put them in food. Later on, for the sake of alacrity I would simply pop them into my mouth without any liquids or food and chew them until I could swallow them.

The only positive thing in my life was sport. Every day after school I would go to my local car park where there was a massive flat wall which I would claim as my own and drill a sliotar off it for thirty minutes a day. I would time myself to make things more scientific. I figured that I was practicing more than anyone else and consequently I would be better than anyone else in matches. There was no effort in doing this daily training. I enjoyed it and could see the results: every match I played for my club and school teams I was playing progressively better, I was being named captain and would play in the centralised positions where traditionally the best players played. The best part of school for me was being let off early to play for the school teams. It was a huge thing for the teacher to stop his lesson and announce to the class that the hurlers or footballers had permission to leave early to play a school match. I would bring my hurl to school every day so that I could practice in the yard before school and at lunch, utilising any free time that was not devoted to the increasing amount of homework and revision we were getting.

When I just turned fifteen I was selected by my club, Scoil Uí Chonaill, to be their representative on the North Dublin boys' trip (with a few football matches) to London. I was definitely not the best player, even on my own team. At that age, your physical attributes, like size and strength, played an enormous part in whether you were considered a good Gaelic footballer. I was very much still growing, lacking both size and strength to dominate games like the other more mature members of my team. However, I did have a fierce work ethic; I always turned up for training and always did my best and I suppose it was these characteristics that tipped the balance in my favour when the mentors sat down and decided who should make the squad for the trip.

There were four or five training sessions before the trip, which allowed the players to mingle and get to know each other. The panel was big, around thirty, and because there was going to be a number of matches played, everyone would be guaranteed a significant amount of game time. Some of the guys on the panel knew me from playing club games against one another but again I was worried about those who did not know me and how I would reveal my stutter to them when I introduced myself or began a conversation. This time, the guys were a little bit more mature; they knew from the training sessions I could look after myself and there were never any overt comments about my speech (at least to my face). Everyone was eager to play for Dublin, enjoy the wonderful experience and secretly hope that it was the start of representing your county for a long time to come.

I don't recall having any particular problems with my speech on the trip but because my social skills were poor from my avoidance behaviours and inherently shy nature I felt on edge throughout the weekend. We took the ferry to Holyhead and a coach to London to stay at a religious college in Ruislip for three nights where we would play a series of challenge games against a number of Irish Gaelic football clubs which had underage boys' teams in their ranks. I remember we won the games fairly easily; I even bagged a few goals over the course of the games, which boosted my confidence amongst the other players and management. I started to come out of my shell more and got to know more of the fellas, a couple of whom continued to represent Dublin up along to grades to senior intercounty level.

My father and eldest sister met me at Dún Laoghaire on my return. My father knew the results of the games from reading recent newspaper articles that had covered the matches and was delighted for me. It was a huge personal challenge to undertake the journey given that the memories of the Belfast trip still weighed heavily on my mind. However, it was important I went and challenged my stammering mentality. Every fibre in my body wanted to refuse to go and allow my comfort zones to shrink further. Despite this, I knew this was a fantastic opportunity and I pushed myself into a situation where I was uncomfortable because the reward was so great. It was an early lesson on how to deal with potential avoidance behaviours and a lesson that I would have to learn many times over the course of my life.

The hurling and football were progressing nicely in secondary school too. Despite having some trouble getting a first team place in first and second year, I physically grew a significant amount in third year and the mentors were confident enough that I could sustain the physical challenges that accompany playing against older students. I was lucky to be involved in a number of very capable teams while in O'Connell CBS and we played a couple of matches in Croke Park, winning some silverware along the way. My practice had paid off; I was one of the prominent players and settled well amongst the groups of genuine guys I played with in secondary school.

Every day there would be either a match or training, which suited me, as it allowed me to spend time out of the house and cleared the head after a full day of classes. My mother had to wash my gear every day and there was always a hot meal when you came home from whichever part of Dublin you were playing your match in. I didn't understand it at the time but I took my mother for granted and was overly judgemental of her and her perceived failings in dealing with my father. I could not have continued to do well in school and sport without the moral and financial support of both my parents.

My confidence and sense of self would simultaneously rise and fall due to the successes in school and sport and the inevitable rows at home. There was never any middle ground, never any moments of quiet reflection and self-satisfaction. Every high was followed by an inevitable low. My speech would be solid with the guys in the yard but desperate when answering a question in class. Outside of school, my speech was unpredictable. I had good days and bad days, but always and consistently when I needed to speak well I could not. When going for a haircut I had to point at the sign for a short back and sides. My mother arranged all doctors' and dentists' appoint-ments even when I was in my late teens. I had severe problems with my name, the 'd' and the 'b' plosive sounds and would be guaranteed to stutter and block for a significant amount of time if ever I was asked for my name. Getting booked in a match was a nightmare too. In order to circumvent any potential problems I would simply give a fictitious name that I could enunciate and calmly jog away from the referee, tremendously self-satisfied with my ingenious ability to disguise my disability. It was such avoidance behaviours that perpet-uated my stammering into adulthood.

Despite the precarious state of my parents' marriage, my sister Elizabeth arrived on the scene when I was fourteen. The pregnancy was difficult for my mother and I remember her having frequent visits to the hospital. Everyone doted on Elizabeth and my other sisters were delighted to have a real-life doll to play with. The dynamic of the household was changing. Space was at a premium and the little flat in Mountain View Court was bursting at the seams.

There was no one in the flats any more whom I could call a friend. Most of my earlier playmates negotiated other paths that inevitably led to involvement in crime or drugs. My parents were worried about the precarious environment and it became harder to sleep at night with the constant police sirens and the screeching tyres of robbed cars under my window. Gangs of teenagers would prowl the walkways and common areas of the flats and drug use was common and more worryingly visible. My parents applied to the Corporation again for a change in accommodation but apparently the waiting lists were full of similarly determined families wanting a safer environment in which to rear their children.

One night after drifting off to the sound of another joyrider being chased by numerous police cars, I awoke to the sight of my father frantically ushering us out of the flat. There was a fetid smell of smoke and burning in the air. The empty apartment directly below us in the complex had been set on fire. It had quickly caught fire and threatened to envelop the whole block. My father, who had been sleeping downstairs at the time, was first to react. Having determined that we were in imminent danger he quickly awoke the family and guided us through the front door to safety from the odorous smoke and flames beginning to lick the front door frame.

I remember rushing out my bedroom door, still in my pyjamas, and grabbing my coat, which was hanging in the hallway. We scurried out into the common areas and watched on as the apartment below ours was engulfed in flames and our little home became increasingly in danger from fire and smoke damage.

The fire brigade came, drawing a huge crowd, and we looked on as they undertook the task of putting out the blaze. One of the neighbours took us in but I don't remember going to bed. I think we stayed up for the remainder of the night, reliving the experience and thinking about our little home. My father had a long discussion with the fire brigade and they assured us there was only limited smoke damage, there was no damage to the structural integrity and that we could return to our home.

Most of the damage was confined to our balcony, which contained the remains of charred washing lines, clothes and unfortunately my first pair of Nike Air runners. My parents re-affirmed their desire to move house to Dublin Corporation and with the added assistance of the local TD they negotiated another successful move. This time we were going to make the slightly longer four-minute journey up the road to Portland Row.

The transition was especially easy for me. In the morning I set off to school from Mountain View Court and then made the afternoon trip after school to Portland Row. My father and mother did all the necessary moving of appliances and furniture while my only responsibilities extended to taking care of my hurleys and football gear, school books and some trophies I had picked up along the way. Everything was taken care of.

The house in Portland Row was just up from the Five Lamps on Amiens Street and may as well have been a million miles from Mountain View Court. The house was three-storey with a front and (tiny) back garden. The structure of the house was important but much more relevant was the atmosphere in the immediate surrounding area. There were no gangs of teenagers prowling. You still had to keep your wits about you but there was no longer that malignant obvious malevolent threat to your personal safety as there was in Mountain View Court.

The move was important because it triggered something in my father. He had always hated living in the flats and, although still technically not his, he had provided his family with a house (not a flat), with a front and back garden, ample space for everyone, with hope and possibilities for the future. He spent much of this time decorating, improving, renovating and cultivating the house in the manner that he had obviously been planning in his head for a long time. I didn't mind the constant smell of new paint in the house as long as it kept him pre-occupied and off my case.

Like most guys of my age I started to notice girls in a meaningful way. Being in an all-boys Christian Brothers school limited your access to the opposite sex tremendously. The other guys on the team would share stories about their romantic exploits on the team bus and before and after games in the dressing room. Everyone secretly knew it was all contrived bullshit but it was entertaining nonetheless. I was convinced that any girl who heard me speak would be instantly repulsed and I would end up as a bitter hermit. I knew that the whole dating process was at least going to have to be a bit different for me. The guys would sometimes go to clubs and latterly bars as we got older but that, at least while I was in school, did not interest me greatly. Puberty had not fully enveloped me yet and besides, most of our matches were played on a Sunday morning. It seemed madness to me to sabotage your performance on a Sunday morning because of a heavy night out on Saturday. By the time we were sixteen or seventten some of the guys were experimenting with drink and getting into bars with fake IDs. I did not share this interest but sometimes the guys insisted and on the very rare occasions I did go out I was disgusted by the taste of alcohol but intrigued by their success rate with women. My social skills were still very poor; my stammer prevented me from having the confidence to approach girls and, at that time, girls were not as progressive or confident enough as they appear today to take the initiative with a guy they liked.

Some guys really enjoyed the social aspect of going out and having a few drinks. According to my mother my father was a big drinker before I was born, but when he gave up drink he reiterated his belief to us that drink was very damaging, it changed people's personalities and had no redeeming qualities. He encouraged us to steer well clear of the stuff as we were growing up and there was never any alcohol in the house, even though my mother likes a glass of beer now and again.

I was intrigued however by the effects alcohol had on my self-confidence and social inhibitions. Even a small quantity of beer would make the music sound better, the conversation more stimulating and create the possibility that tonight I might actually talk to a girl. When you stammer, you carry emotional baggage with you everywhere you go. That baggage is relieved from you when you have alcohol. Physically you are less likely to hold back in your thoughts and speaking processes. Holding back is one of the building blocks for stammering. You want to speak but you know you physically can't. You are still in an apparent conflict. The desire to speak is matched with the fear of speaking. Hence the creation of a speech block.

But if the equation shifts a little, and the desire to speak is elevated with a consequence reduction in the fear of speaking then we are on to something, then we begin to let go of inhibitions. The quality of the content of your speech cannot be guaranteed but you do become more loquacious when you have had a drink or two. I would make practical use of this realisation a number of times when I was in college. My problem was that I did not enjoy the taste of drink; the alcohol increased the severity and frequency of my headaches; and the periods of inhibited free speech were fleeting and increasingly hard to attain.

By sixteen I was playing senior hurling for my club. It was intimidating at first to be playing with and against grown men. The training sessions were rudimentary but very effective and always involved a lengthy match. These matches were pivotal in educating me on how to protect and look after myself on the hurling pitch and at that time there were still some very good hurlers on the team to look up to, admire and copy. I was involved in minor, under-21 and now senior teams with my club and invariably I had two matches at the weekends. When you consider my involvement with the school and associated training sessions, I was hurling or playing football every day. The constant participation in sports kept my mind from focusing on my self-constructed negative thoughts. All other free time was spent studying, doing homework or thinking about the next match.

I was selected for trials for the Dublin minor hurling team and did reasonably well considering I had hurled with a dislocated finger for most of the trial game. I knew a few of the lads who were guaranteed starters and they were encouraging but I didn't think I had done enough to justify my selection. In that time there was an A and a B panel and as expected I made the B panel. I had been a little naive in the trial game, laying the ball off to people and not being ruthless enough in the tackle. I swore to myself that if ever I was involved in another trial match I would break free of the shackles and let go.

We played Wicklow in our one and only match that year. We lost and I had just a few minutes game time. The structures were not as sophisticated as they are now. We were given tea and biscuits at the post-match reception, thanked for our efforts and told to keep hurling away and improve. Seemed sensible enough advice to me.

I had been thinking about my steps after school for a long time and wanted to go to college in the hope of bettering myself and obtaining a higher standard of living than I had grown up with. We never starved or wanted for anything but I did not want to have to endure the same financial pressure and stress that my father did. I wanted to be successful and have a professional career, have continuous prospects and advancement opportunities and be excited on a daily basis about going to work. My stammer constantly weighed on my mind and that was a huge factor in my decision-making process in considering what career I was going to choose and also what course I was going to apply for in college. I could not afford to attend third-level education outside of Dublin; there were simply insufficient funds for that so for the moment I was stuck at home. I considered getting a part-time job in college in order to fund a potential move away from home but that would involve having to speak to strangers, step outside my comfort zones and challenge my stammer. I retreated and backed down. I rationalised that a part-time job would jeopardise my studies, preventing me from attending all the lectures and diminishing the whole college experience. I wanted to leave home but was too scared and immature to take those steps.

When the time came to consider third-level options I realised I had still some work to do in order to achieve the required points for the courses that interested me. My performances were solid in school and I knew that if I worked smart and consistently, and approached the final few months giving everything I had, then there would be no problem. Fifth and sixth year was all about gearing up for the Leaving Cert. The teachers were focused and encouraging and pushed everyone to maximise their potential. There would be frequent assessments, revision sessions, exam technique sessions and there was a genuine competition in the class to see who were the top dogs and get the highest points. My favourite subjects were all numerical based – Maths, Physics, Applied Maths – but I also liked Accounting and English. I struggled with the languages because I don't have a natural flair for them. I had good vocabulary and could structure and construct sentences and read comprehension but I was a very ordinary language student. I was hoping to get most of my points based on my interest in Maths and the maths-based subjects.

As a boy I was interested in engines and airplanes and considered engineering as a possible career choice. I liked Accounting though and weighed that career option up against engineering. All things being equal, I factored into the equation my stammer and determined that accountants would have less necessity for oral communication and in fact could actually be quite successful being silently fed work in faceless offices where no one spoke to one another. I would not say that my stammer was *the* all-defining factor in my decision to study Accounting and Finance at DCU but it certainly made its presence felt when I rolled the dice. Later on in my life I would look back and reflect on whether I had made the correct choice but it wasn't long before my decision was made and I began to work towards my desired goal of becoming an accountant.

The first major hurdles were the oral exams in Irish and French. My speech was disastrous in the lead-up and the added pressure of there being an academic consequence of not being fluent was enough to nearly unhinge me. I prepared as best I could, practiced out loud on my own, in front of the mirror and while walking to school in the morning. I knew the designated phrases and responses, was confident in my ability to understand any potential questions and I had the vocabulary to at least answer a pertinent response. However, every time I opened my mouth in those exams, nothing, and I mean nothing, came out. The silences grew as the exam wore on, the blocks would last seconds, then minutes, as the perspiration flowed down my temples. I knew what responses I should be giving but my speech process would not deliver. I was too nervous, too distracted, too self-aware of my own inability to speak and only too aware of the horrified expression on the examiner's face when he saw me in mid-block. When the process was over (for both exams, Irish and French) I resigned myself to the fact that I had failed and that I could not expect a passing grade when the examiner had absolutely no material to work with and correct. I believe that my teachers had spoken to the examiners prior to the exams but in all honesty there was nothing they could do. I consoled myself with the fact that for the rest of the year I could focus on my written work but I knew that I had let myself down and also the teachers down for all the hard work they had put into our class and the encouragement they had shown me.

About a month before the Leaving Certificate started, there was a graduation ceremony where our class and all the other sixth year classes gathered to celebrate five years (there was no transition year) in secondary school and for us officially becoming ex-students. There was a real sense of occasion that night as the parents accompanied the students to the ceremony. All the teaching staff were in attendance and the school hall had a different dynamic that night. For the past five years the relationship was distinctly teacher and student for everyone and those roles could not be breached. However that night all the teachers greeted us warmly and there was an unusual friendliness and sense of camaraderie pervasive in the school hall. They all seem genuinely delighted that we had made it to sixth year and that they had done everything they could to prepare us for the Leaving Certificate coming up. I was sitting there in my oversized light blue jacket and light grey trousers, hoping that there would no occasion where I would have to speak when the principal rose, made his way to the makeshift lectern and prepared to announce the Student of the Year. For me, secondary school had been about endurance, about consistently being uncomfortable, about feeling fear and marching on, irrespective of the speech blocks I had or the times I held my head in shame because of my failed attempts to communicate. It was also about the friendships made, the pride I felt when I wore the school jersey and the adulation we earned when we walked around the school with the trophy our team had just won. It was about toughening me up, taking knocks and seeing if I would stay down on the floor or get up and go again. I certainly wasn't the brightest in the class but I worked to the best of my ability and every day was a challenge for me. I had made some good friends along the way who for the vast majority of my school days were supportive and understanding, and treated me like anyone else. I think that is why I was selected Student of the Year. I had understood what the teachers were trying to do; I had difficulties for the first three years with a couple of teachers but I had earned their respect by never giving in.

The only drawback of getting the award was the pressure it put on me to achieve a good Leaving Certificate. The pressure was mostly self-imposed. For the remaining time to the exams I finessed my notes and exam technique, focused on relaxation and visualisation, and felt ready and confident to achieve my potential. The principal had told our class that our first attempt at something was always our best one and I was determined not to have to go through this experience again. I was virtually a recluse in my room and the hurling and football were wound down significantly. The risk of breaking a finger or wrist and not being able to write was just too great. Every night to relax after studying I would listen to the REM album *Automatic for the People* and fall asleep by the time 'Find the River' ended.

By the following August I achieved the grades that I had wanted and felt a surge of satisfaction and relief. All that hard work had paid off. On the morning of the results we had to return to school and individually obtain our exam grades. All the teachers were there to share our success or console us if we missed our mark. I was excited about telling my parents and about sharing my results with everyone else. All my friends had done well. Everyone was taking their first steps in starting their new careers.

The realisation that I would be going to DCU dawned on me, and the familiar stammering mentality of pre-event tension and anxiety resurfaced. I would have to meet new people. I would have to introduce myself. In all probability, I would have to do class presentations. I would have to participate in tutorials. More worryingly, the audience this time would not just be friends, fellow hurlers or classmates but would include girls! How would they react to my stammering behaviours, my blocks, my tricks and avoidances?

Better than expected, as it turned out.

4

University – The Undergraduate Years

I had spent most of the morning I was supposed to be leaving for DCU for orientation frantically trying on my limited selection of clothes, trying to appear effortlessly cool on my first day in third-level education. I was racked with nervous tension, excitement and foreboding. I made the bicycle journey up Dorset Street, through Drumcondra and then Collins Avenue to DCU in September 1993.

I was determined to embrace everything that DCU offered and was keen to know more details about the Accounting and Finance course I had selected, the strength of the hurling team and the other amenities that the colourful brochures advertised. The first stop was the Larkin Theatre, which is a large circular-shaped lecture hall in the middle of campus. The entire contingent of first-year students gathered there and were formally welcomed by the university president. All the seats had been taken by the time I filed in and I stood at the very back, coolly leaning against the wall, pretending to be centred and self-assured, and inwardly praying that I would not have to introduce myself to anyone today. The president began his speech, detailed the academic successes and developments of the university and wrapped things up by wishing us the very best of luck. He then inevitably asked everyone to introduce themselves to the people to their immediate right and left. He thereby surmised that everyone would have at least two other individuals to talk to and roam the campus with on their collective first days.

I composed myself enough to introduce myself, with some difficulty, to someone who was actually doing the same course as me. He was standing to my right. It was such an effort to complete the first introduction that I failed to complete my second one. I pretended to not notice the outstretched hand of my potential colleague to my left, shuffled off down the stairs and congratulated myself for avoiding another painful speaking experience. My self-appreciation, which was a deluded consequence of my cowardice, had conquered my embarrassment.

I latched on to my fellow classmate as we wandered around the campus, listening to an eclectic mix of current students and faculty members extolling the virtues of DCU. My responses to his questions and comments were guarded, monosyllabic and, in the majority, fiction. I tailored my answers so that I used the very limited words I could say without stammering.

Later, after a complimentary burger and chips in the canteen (this was to be the staple diet of the vast percentage of first-year students for the 1993/1994 academic year), all new Accounting and Finance students were asked to attend a brief lecture by the head of the Accounting programme in one of the lecture halls in the Business School. I somehow sensed that there would be talking involved, my pre-event premonition abilities working overtime. I internally debated whether to return home, patrol the campus alone or stand outside and listen with my ear to the door. I worked out the odds and determined that in all probability there was a very slim chance I would have to talk. How unlucky could I be? He could not ask everyone to speak, could he?

We nosily filled the lecture hall and I guessed that sitting somewhere in the middle would be the safest place to avoid having to speak. The lecturer appeared to be the stereotypical accountant: middle-aged, spectacles, thinning hair, slightly overweight, and with a variety of pens in the top pocket of a crease-riddled white shirt.

He gave some basic information about the course and himself and I was impressed by his academic qualifications and the number of letters after his name. He then smiled and eagerly announced that he would like to get to know a bit about everyone in his class. My adrenaline spiked sharply. Here we go, I thought. This is the big reveal. This is where everyone in your year will know that you are a stutterer. My negative self-talk began in earnest: be prepared for the sniggers and sideways looks and the start of three years of constant abuse.

Starting at the back of the class, everyone was asked to state their name, where they came from and what secondary school they had attended. Anybody with a normal-sized brain and cognitive ability would find this a redundant exercise as, after five students, each successive name, address and school would fade from memory. But not this lecturer. He had letters before *and* after his name. He was going to actually remember everyone and he was definitely going to remember me. I felt I was back in school, in History and Geography class, waiting for my time to speak and just knowing, knowing, that I would fail miserably and lapse into prolonged and obvious stuttering. I thought about getting up and leaving. Can't – there's tens of students to my left and right. What a rookie mistake! You would have thought I should have known where to position myself in a room full of strangers by now. Feign a heart attack? Fainting? That could work ... *but* it would also bring unwanted attention to me. No ... just think ... think .... The clock was ticking. Everyone was confidently giving their details to approving nods by the lecturer as he was carefully classifying and storing the data into the vast recesses of his cavernous mind. Jesus Christ, what am I going to do? Say another name ... yes, that's it ... no one here knows me. Yes ... no wait ... someone does – the guy I introduced myself to in the Larkin Theatre. Fuck. I should have lied back there too.

A hushed silence fell on the room. The metaphorical axe had been raised and was hovering over my outstretched neck. It was my time to speak. Jesus Christ. I was shaking, my trembling left leg rhythmically hitting the underside of the table like a snare drum. All eyes started to fall upon me. My colleague from the Larkin Theatre lowered his gaze and turned his head away. 'Darren Benham, from Dublin. I went to O'Connell CBS.' These were the words I *wanted* to come out of my mouth. I wanted to announce my presence to the entire class, confidently, succinctly, with clear intention and purpose. I wanted everyone to know I meant business; I was serious about my grades; I was going to be on the hurling team; and I had that self-belief and inner resolve that girls find interesting, even attractive. I wanted to be that guy.

The sounds that actually came out of my strangled vocal chords were more like 'aren ham, O'nells, lin.' I lowered my head and counted the seconds. Five. Eight. Ten. I looked up and the lecturer held my gaze while the next student took up the baton. I shrugged my shoulders. I had done what I could. Thinking back, I would have avoided going to the lecture if I had known what was about to occur and I would have gladly missed out on key knowledge about the impending lectures, continuous assessments and prescribed reading materials. I had somehow gotten through the experience with another bumbling performance and cursed myself for not having the ability to communicate like everyone in the class. I knew that some people were feeling tension too but theirs was a different tension. I cared what people thought of me. I genuinely wanted people *not* to think of stammering when they first thought about me. It was a tough start but a salutary lesson that now, at least I *really* needed to do something about the way I talked. Needless to say, I did nothing about it.

The first day of official term started and the lectures came thick and fast. My course was only a three-year one with an option to continue to do a Masters if your grades were adequate and your intention strong enough. There was this awkward feeling-out process for everyone, trying to associate with similar type people, perhaps from the same city or town. Groups started to grow organically. I fell in with a group of similarly ambitious guys from Dublin which later expanded to include a couple of lads from Donegal. After a while there were clearly defined pockets of individuals scattered around the lecture halls, all huddled in their groups, finding strength in numbers and preparing to face the trials of first semester exams while at the same time experiencing the unique social life that college life offers. At that time, the big student night was Thursday in the DCU bar, as evidenced by the meagre attendance at lectures on a Friday morning. I had training with my club and latterly the

Dublin team on a Thursday so for the first year of college at least my appearances in the bar on a Thursday night were few and far between.

My speech at that time can only be described as bi-polar. When I had to speak in a tutorial or in any formal occasion it was chronic. I reverted to using tricks, like slapping my leg, strangling out sounds or substituting words, or, better still, avoiding where possible. Within my group of friends from college, with the guys from the hurling and football teams, I would appear self-confident and extrovert, all the while scanning ahead for words and gently steering any conversation away from myself and any opinions I would have to give. This display of self-confidence was entirely for self-preservation purposes. I did not want to appear weak or vulnerable to snide comments and so, for most of the time, I presented a fictitious and fraudulent persona in any social situation. Very much like the occasion in primary school when I adopted a country accent, I acted with confidence, I pretended to be self-assured, and in the limited occasions when I did speak I was only competent in short bursts. My physical speaking mechanisms could not sustain fluency for more than three words (and never for words with more than three syllables). It was only later on, with further successes in hurling and football and limited successes with girls, did I get the requisite desired boost in self-confidence to experiment more with my speech, try new things and speak to different people. By this time, I had recognised this tenuous and fleeting correlation between speaking well and having strong positive feelings about myself. However, it was only when I undertook the McGuire Programme, almost ten years later, did I come to understand how important self-belief, self-acceptance and personal happiness is to sustained successful speaking performances.

A couple of weeks after the semester began there was a Clubs and Societies Day where all the university-based clubs and societies advertised for new members. There was only one club I was interested in joining and I eagerly searched out the Hurling Club stand, ready to sign up. At that time, there was a fresher (first-year) team and a senior hurling team and I went to the stand with the basic expectation of getting on the fresher team. I wrote my name down on a list of interested freshers (I was surprised to find that the list was short), committed to memory the time and date of the first trial match, and stuck around a while to check out the potential competition and see who else was involved. Little was known about the fresher team for 1993; it was a case of wait and see who turns up to the trial match. The senior team had a few very strong players and a couple of county players. Seán Power, the then Dublin senior hurling full-back, played centre back on the senior team. Brendan Maher, who hurled senior intercounty for Kildare, played corner-back. Henry Roberts, a former Kilkenny minor, hurled at full-back. Robbie Shortall, the Kilkenny under-21 star, played centre-forward. I was looking forward to the freshers trial game to see how high the standard was and testing myself against a strong University of Limerick first-year team.

The fresher hurlers gathered in the DCU sports complex the following Wednesday afternoon. Everyone was eyeing each other up, assessing one another, trying to figure out who the best players were, where everyone was from and hoping for a coveted jersey. Traditionally, University of Limerick would bring a strong outfit. Danny McGovern was in charge of the team for that day. He was a former DCU player and student and was from Laois, a county – very much like Dublin – that did not have a successful county hurling set-up but was filled with people who had a passionate love for the game. He was also the manager of the DCU senior team and would be keeping an eye out for anyone who could challenge for a place on that team. The names were read aloud from the signing sheet at the Clubs and Societies Day and for some mysterious reason I was selected to play centre-back. My position for my club was wing-back but there were apparently more forwards available for selection than backs and so the managers had to do some reshuffling to generate a balanced team. The match was held on the grounds at the extreme left of the campus on a very uneven and cut-up pitch. In any event I was delighted to be starting though I was a little anxious about being centre-back, which was more of a holding position and neces-sitated constant marking of your man. I was used to a freer role playing wing-back for the club. As expected, UL were strong with some very decent hurlers. I quickly noticed that our standard wasn't great; we had only a few hurlers capable of playing at that level. I was quickly involved early on with a few high catches and clearances. I was competent although certainly not spectacular, but I thoroughly enjoyed my first college match. The result was deemed irrelevant by both teams. Which is one way of saying DCU got hammered. Walking off the pitch I was approached by Danny and he asked me to join the senior squad for training the following Monday night. I didn't even have to think about it. I had achieved my first goal of getting on the panel. The next steps would be to get a place on the starting fifteen and see how things developed.

My relationships at home, especially with my father, continued to be very stressful for me and I used to dread having to spend any time at home whatsoever. The rows and arguments became so frequent that I would just walk out the door and not come back till nighttime. My thoughts during and immediately subsequent to these arguments would be all-consuming and extremely dark. I lost all sense of reason and rationality. I remember after one argument I convinced myself that the only option was to join the French Foreign Legion, an ostensibly French elite armed forces unit but renowned for taking in undesirables from all over the world if you swore allegiance to France. At that time there was a Citizens' Advice Bureau on O'Connell Street, and I decided I was simply going to go in, announce my intention to join the Legion and enrol the next day. I knew that I was going to have to speak to someone in the Citizens' Advice Bureau but I also knew that my speech was at such a low point that I would be incomprehensible. I wrote down exactly what I was going to say on a piece of paper and presented it to the receptionist. I had written that I was a mute and would like to join the Foreign Legion, thank you very much. I had made a silent promise I would never open my mouth again. The kindly receptionist gave me some numbers and addresses and an information leaflet. I walked around town listening to music on my Walkman as I formulated different strategies to progress through life without opening my mouth again. All attempts ultimately proved futile. In every scenario verbal communication was a necessity. It was as if I would abandon all logic and reason during my attempts to deal with and overcome the emotional damage caused by yet another argument. The thought never occurred to me to try further speech therapy. I was definitely resigned to a life governed mercilessly by my stammer. I was not thinking enough *about* my stammer. I didn't try to deconstruct or analyse it. It was simply omnipresent. It was precariously unpredictable. On some occasions

I could talk – in the dressing room, with my college friends – but on other occasions – tutorials, on the phone, with my parents – my speaking process broke down and embarrassed me. That frustrated me but at the time I didn't see any alternatives to the life I was envisaging for myself.

The rest of the college year involved enjoying the lectures, avoiding tutorials where the tutor asked questions, getting familiar with the library and forcing my way onto the senior hurling team. I started to get to know some more people from my class, simply from bumping into them in the library, seeing them in the corridors or canteen, and from very rare social occasions where I would visit the bar.

The senior hurling training was held on a Monday night and was principally running based. There were no quality lights at that time and so everyone spent the hour running around a muddy field trying not to bump into each other. Everyone was starting to get to know one another. The experienced players were welcoming and inclusive and respected you if you did well at training and didn't let the team down during competitive matches. I played midfield for the senior team and centre-back for the freshers team and with all my other club commitments I was playing hurling and football nearly every day of the week. I saw no problem with this and at that age the body is willing and able to oblige. I worked out a regime of lectures, studying and training that suited me and kept me busy and fit and out of the house for as long as possible. Sometimes we would travel to matches to play against other universities and that would involve an all-day trip. It was on these trips that the real bonding began. There would be singing and drinking on the bus, irrespective of the result, messing and slagging, testing each other, and joke- and story-telling. I was fascinated by the lads from the country viewing everyone from Dublin as robbers and thieves with no knowledge or prowess at hurling. There were a few lads from Dublin on the team and we challenged these preconceptions during the matches we played but my case was undone when I told everyone I lived on Portland Row, Summerhill.

We played primarily in near-Artic conditions as the university hurling calendar started in January. Most matches were played with Deep Heat on the hands and long-sleeved shirts underneath the jerseys. The standard of the senior games was deceptively high, practically the same as intercounty level, and though we lost more games than we won I was optimistic about achieving success over the next few years. Our first Fitzgibbon Cup game (third-level hurling championship) was against UCD that year and I ended up marking Johnny Pilkington, the Offaly midfielder. I remember thinking he was the best player I had faced in my life but I needed to try to play my own game, and keep the ball moving and away from him as much as possible. He was incredibly fit and very polished. He never made one mistake and gave us all a lesson. I kept running for the 70 minutes and cleared a few balls but UCD were too strong for us. We were out of all competitions for that year but at least we had something to build on for the next season.

After the match, the boys went on a huge session in the DCU bar with free drink provided by Ciarán Duffy, a legendary figure in DCU folklore. He was a rep for either Guinness or Heineken and student liaison officer (or something to that affect) and current senior player. His exact title was always a bone of contention. He technically was a student but more importantly to us he had a unique ability to supply free kegs of beer after every match. I was still a little hesitant about joining in these marathon drinking sessions. I was not comfortable around drink at that time; I didn't like the taste of it but I enjoyed listening to the boys singing and I liked the way they attracted groups of women to their tables. I admired their self-confidence and ability to let go and enjoy themselves, but I had to break down a few personal barriers and self-imposed inhibitions before I would be comfortable in that sort of environment.

My grades in the Leaving Certificate and attendance at DCU qualified me for an AIB scholarship for those attending DCU from the inner city. I don't recall any money being involved but there was the opportunity of a summer job, if I wanted it, in AIB Investment Managers in Percy Place, near Baggot Street. I was terrified about the prospect of the job, having to reveal my stutter yet again to strangers, and only thought about the negatives of this unique opportunity. There was no interview and no orientation process. I would just turn up one Monday morning, announce myself and become gainfully employed by AIB. I had to carefully decide whether I wanted to accept the opportunity and embrace it or retreat into my comfort zone and spend the summer walking the streets, listening to REM, trying to stay out of my father's way.

I rationalised that I would only be a summer intern and therefore not entrusted with anything of importance, and, in all probability, I would be stuck in some filing room on my hands and knees sorting post or shredding documents. I also surmised that the money would come in very handy and at least give me some defence to my father's argument that he was working his ass off just to keep me in college. I reluctantly rang the lady in charge of the scholarship programme and, after about 20 minutes of barely comprehensible stammering, confirmed my acceptance and gratefully hung up with about 50 unanswered questions in my head. Do I wear a suit? How much will I get paid? Will I be able to go home early for matches?

On my arrival at Percy Place I presented the main receptionist with my acceptance letter, deliberately pointing at my name written on the page to ensure she knew who I was, and nervously waited for one of the secretaries from the Investment Managers Department to meet me, bring me to where I would be working and introduce me to my future colleagues. The introductions would have to be her responsibility.

I spent most of my summer there, as expected sorting out files, shredding, doing some Excel work, going to the shop, getting lunches, proofreading memos and totting up columns of figures on a spectacularly noisy calculator. My colleagues were pleasant, unassuming, self-confident and evidently very capable. My department handled privately held investments, principally investments held by high net worth individuals, and over time I got to know some of the terminology regularly used. It was a positive learning experience in that I got to know what working in an office was like, how sometimes working in a team can be challenging and simultaneously rewarding, and experiencing first-hand the pressures associated with month-end accounts and demanding superiors. My verbal interactions were monosyllabic, which suited me, and the most I had to talk in a day was when I had to go to the shop for the lunchtime sandwiches. Although that was very much truncated as I simply presented my immaculately handwritten shopping list to the shop assistant and smiled expectantly.

From my careful observations, the most important and diligent people in my department were the secretaries, who kept their bosses informed, on time, up to date and on their toes. They knew all the gossip in the place (which they would eagerly share with you) and they always seemed to work the hardest.

I got to know a couple of the other interns working in Percy Place too. They were mostly related to current employees and very often had worked there previously and already knew the ropes. They were streetwise and confident and exuded a pungent air of superiority. But they still had to do the shredding like me.

By the time I started second year of college, puberty had belatedly kicked in. I suddenly began to notice the girls in my class and in the other classes and throughout the college. It amazed me that they had not preoccupied my thoughts previously, given their close proximity. I knew I would never have the courage to simply approach someone who caught my eye and introduce myself. The structure and plosive sounds of my name rendered every attempt I had at enunciating it disastrous. No, I had to find another method of getting to know girls. I tried to come up with a plan that allowed me to get to know someone without the ordeal of having to physically say my name as an introduction and instantly reveal my stutter to them. Help came in the form of the greatest hurler I ever played with.

The DCU hurling team got stronger the second year I was on it principally because of the arrival of Johnny Sheehan. He was a former Cork minor underage star, who played senior club hurling in Cork. I first met him at a DCU training session. He was physically the same size and stature as me and like all Cork people seemed easy-going, laconic and filled with an unjustified self-confidence. In his case, however, it was blatantly justified. He didn't just hit a ball. He cajoled it to do what he wanted. He was wristy, wiry, tough, athletic and balletic, and could make the ball talk. He had a huge jump and even when surrounded by three or four markers he could catch a ball from the air and deliver it to where the forwards like it most: to the wing and bouncing up in front of them. He was singularly the most talented and naturally gifted player I had ever seen. And he was playing for DCU that year.

After a few training sessions, where I desperately tried to mark him in practice games, we got to talking, shared stories about our clubs, where we were from and what we thought of DCU. He was doing one of the science courses and was living with a number of guys directly across the road from campus. He was intrigued about what hurling in Dublin was like given the poor performances of the county team generally at that time. He was very knowledgeable about the game and after matches he would sit in the bar and tell stories about the Cork championship, who was impressing him and what teams he expected to be successful in that year's All-Ireland series. He went on to win an All-Ireland medal with Cork in 1999 as a substitute.

Everyone called him Johnny Star. The name suited him. He would regularly be the star attraction when the competitive matches began and all the boys knew that when they got the ball the best chance of a score would come if the ball would be delivered up his wing. Ostensibly he played wing-forward but he moved where he wanted to in the forwards. He was great at reading the game, knowing where the ball would land and positioning himself correctly. During many matches I would feed the ball to him and watch him strike it over the bar with his incredibly wristy strike, thinking that someday he was going to be one of the greatest of all time.

Star loved hurling but he embraced the social side too. After matches he would invariably be found in the bar, his housemates and other teammates around him, enjoying the pints that came courtesy of Ciarán Duffy. He was sensationally charismatic and made everyone feel included and worthwhile. When all the boys got together it was something to see. The pints would flow and the singing would start. Rebel songs. County songs. Oasis. Pearl Jam. Whatever popped into their heads. Then, inevitably as the night wore on, the respective girlfriends would arrive, and their friends, and *their* friends, until a huge group of people, centred on the hurlers, would congregate in the middle of the bar and take over the place.

By this time, however, I was no longer jealously looking in. Star would grab me, tell me to sit with the lads and order me a drink; we would talk hurling and in particular DCU hurling and how we were going to win every competition we were part of for as long as we were in college. I was introduced to his housemates, his current girlfriend and her friends, and so I had bypassed the formal introductions stage simply because of my association with Johnny Sheehan.

My self-esteem, confidence and self-belief were slowly undergoing positive changes as a result of my interactions with and within the various hurling and football teams I was playing with. This, coupled with a reduction in my overall time spent at home under the influence of my father, resulted in an improvement in my speech amongst my peers and group of friends. I always had this dichotomy in my speech. When I needed it to be good, for example on the phone or simply giving my name formally, I struggled a lot but I found I could hold and maintain a conversation with friends once I was relaxed and, most importantly, felt included and self-assured. This came about principally from the happiness I obtained playing for the college. I was pushing for a place on the county panel, I was hurling well with my club and I was handling the increased academic requirements that second year demanded.

I would still beat myself up about my negative speaking experiences and spend a lot of time reflecting on these failures as opposed to focusing on the increasing number of positives in my life. It was frustrating to obtain fleeting glimpses of fluency in the bar after a match and still have to point at the sign where it said 'short back and sides' when going to the barbers.

From the start of third year I felt secure enough within the extended hurling group of players and associated girlfriends and other friends to begin to enjoy getting to know girls. I enjoyed my limited conversations with them. I found that even a little alcohol relaxed me to the point where I could spend an entire evening chatting to a girl, getting to know her. The alcohol certainly reduced my inhibitions and negative perceptions about my stutter. It relaxed me. It brought me closer to the extended group. It enabled me to experience something of what it would be like to be a normal, fluent speaker, free from the constant thoughts of stammering, of speech blocks, post-event self-hate and shame and the ever-present pre-event anxiety and tension. I liked the feeling but even then I knew it was fleeting and transient. I had no affection for the taste; it increased the frequency of my headaches and it just was not *me*. It enabled me to bypass certain initial hurdles, particularly the difficulty I had with my name, and it brought me that false confidence that tricked my brain into thinking I could be interesting and attractive to the women I found attractive amongst the group.

Looking back, I don't think there was a physiological reason why my speech became more fluent after a couple of drinks. I believe that it simply altered the overly self-analytical personality I have and that I was less afraid to make a mistake or more specifically less afraid of having a physical speech block while talking when I was drinking. Again, it was not until I joined the McGuire Programme that I recognised that a physical speech block is very often the end result of simply having a deeply ingrained fear of the physical act of stammering itself. In my case, most of the fear I had before speaking revolved around the potential consequences I envisaged would occur if I demonstrably displayed a physical speech block or a noticeable bouncing or struggle with a sound. When I was drinking I seemed to just not care about the potential consequences and therefore most of my fears simply dissolved away (inevitably leading to more fluent speech).

To my great surprise, any interactions with women in DCU were entirely positive and affirming. There was never any mention of my speech nor any negative reaction to a single speech block I had. All of the women I became involved with, either socially or in brief relationships, never once mentioned it to me in a derogatory manner, or brought it up as something that irritated them or even as a curiosity to be discussed and examined. They were united in their understanding and empathy towards me and surprised me with their genuineness. All the pre-event anxiety I had built up in my life regarding future possible interactions with women were dispelled while I was in college.

The DCU senior hurling team in my third year was shaping up to be the strongest yet. There was an influx of quality players from Cork and Wexford that immediately boosted the panel. The main attraction was Seán Óg Ó hAilpín, the Cork dual star who had just performed miracles in the minor hurling All-Ireland final that September. Danny McGovern was once again in charge and I remember Seán Óg's first game for the seniors. I was playing wing-back and he was centre-back and we were playing Mary Immaculate College in Limerick. I was busy enough marking my own man but one time I looked across at Seán Óg and he was an unusually long distance off his man, either to the side or behind him, eyes carefully focused on the ball. I screamed at him to mark his man. He looked over at me and simply nodded. When the ball did come his man's way, Seán Óg glided up through his gears, made up the space between him and his player, dispossessed him and drove the ball sixty yards up the pitch. I didn't scream at him again.

There was an innocence and purity about him which contrasted with the wild charisma and bombastic nature of Johnny Star. He was incredibly humble and dedicated, and he trained and played like a professional. He was a huge addition to the team, effortlessly slotting into the centre-back position, and, with Johnny Star now playing centre-forward in the team, there was a greater sense of balance and cohesion in the way we played. We had lost a few of the older players but this group seemed fitter and keener for success than any previous team. We trained diligently and made the league finals that year but were beaten (I think) by an Athlone IT team that contained the mercurial future Galway star Kevin Broderick.

The trips and matches away were immensely entertaining and memorable, and though Seán Óg did not drink we more than made up for his sobriety. He never excluded himself from the post-match celebrations however and often would be the first to sing a song and rally the troops when the proceedings were beginning to die down. Everyone knew that he was going to be one of the greatest of the game, even at that age.

In early 1996 I took my first steps in becoming a senior inter-county hurler. I was awarded an *Evening Herald* Dublin Club Hurler of the Month award for February after a series of good displays for my club. It was this award that brought me to the attention of the county management team. The award necessitated that I attend a function and a dinner with the comparative football recipient and a selection of GAA journalists who wrote for the papers. I did not attend the event on account of my lack of confidence in my speech. I told the organisers that I had college commitments when instead I was locked in my room within my shrinking comfort zones. My club hurling manager attended the function in my place and was duly photographed in the *Evening Herald* enjoying the free meal and scintillating conversation.

I was informed by my club that I was to attend a trial county game against Kilkenny that month. I was accompanied by a fellow club-mate, Gavin O'Donoghue, a precocious talent who had himself been playing very well for the club. He had played minor county football for Dublin and in my opinion was a better footballer than hurler but he was an unpredictable and spectacular talent who could embarrass his marker in a multitude of ways. We made our way to a pub in Rathcoole which was to be the meeting point for the main bunch of players who were taking the bus to a club venue in Kilkenny. We were anxious not to be late for our intercounty debuts and inevitably ended up being early and sitting in the bar, sipping water, surrounded by our gear and hurleys with new grips on them. Slowly the other players began to arrive. My lack of confidence and self-belief was ably countered by Gavin's enthusiasm and faith in his own ability. He confidently explained to everyone who would listen that the Dublin management had specifically organised the meeting to assess *his* inevitable progression to the county team. For anyone else this would be hubris, but Gavin had the ability to back up his claims.

I remember the special feeling putting on my first senior county jersey and thinking 'this feels right'. I had not told my family about the match; I was determined not to jeopardise my wavering self-confidence and happiness with a potential argument with my father. He was aware that I would be away from the house all day but as far as he was aware I was away at a college match.

I was not acquainted with anybody on the team, apart from Gavin, but I recognised the majority of them from their pictures in the newspaper and seeing some of them hurl for Dublin on the television. I was intimidated, overawed and praying that I would not make a serious mistake that would cost us the game or indeed incur the wrath of my teammates. Everyone, however, was welcoming and told me just to play my own game and do my best. I tried to settle myself. We were about to play in atrocious conditions; there was incessant rain and a biting wind that brought the temperature down a couple of degrees.

When we took to the field I automatically tried to locate the presence of the more famous faces from the Kilkenny team over the previous number of years: DJ Carey, John Power, Eamon Morrissey. Unfortunately they were all absent; Kilkenny were apparently treating the game like Dublin were – trying out up-and-coming players and seeking out anyone who could enhance their respective panels before the start of the Leinster championship.

The conditions brought the standard of hurling to an almost farcical level. The rain was heavy and constant, soaking everyone, and made gripping the handle of the hurley tenuous at best. I remember running around frantically in my left-half-forward position, trying to close down men, seeking a hook and a block to get myself into the game. I spent most of the game sliding on the wet grass.

When the match concluded we huddled into the dressing rooms and were addressed by the then manager, Jimmy Gray. We were all told that it was unfair to judge anyone's hurling abilities in these conditions and that we would be individually contacted with a view to organising further trial matches or training sessions in order for us to be more judiciously assessed as potential intercounty hurlers.

It was an enjoyable experience to have broken the ice with the current crop of senior Dublin players. There was some conversation between the other players and Gavin and I during the journey home but we mostly kept to ourselves, trying to internalise how we performed. I think Gavin played right-half-forward that day and, like me, struggled with the conditions. He probably did a little better than me but I was happy I would have another chance, hopefully in more favourable conditions, to express myself and prove I was good enough for the panel.

For the next few months my life was consumed with hurling, studying for my finals and staying out of the house. I was asked to join the under-21 county hurling panel for their first match against Offaly, in Tullamore. I knew a couple of guys from the panel, simply from playing regularly against them in club games and a couple of them I knew from playing with and against them while playing for DCU. I had not attended any prior training sessions and effectively turned up at the side of the pitch with my gear. I did not start the match. As I recall the game was very even and score followed opposing score. I came on in the second half in midfield and just concentrated on keeping the ball moving into our forward line. We drew the match but in fairness either side could had claimed the spoils that day.

A month later I was asked by the senior management team to come to a training session where there would be a trial match between the current A team and potential new recruits to the panel. Again, I was selected in midfield and performed well, catching a few balls as well as putting a few over the bar. I was confident after the match that I had done enough to justify my selection but coming from a small club you always felt a little disadvantaged while in the county set-up. As I was getting changed, readying myself to go home, Jimmy Gray approached me and coolly asked me whether I would be interested in joining the panel. 'Yes', I stammered, 'very much so.' There was no grandiose sense of self-satisfaction or achievement. The personal satisfaction I had felt on joining the senior county panel was measured and contained because it was countered by my natural tendency to construct negatives and limiting beliefs around potential positive experiences. I was immediately thinking about the pressures associated with playing county: the quality of the opposi-tion, the competition for places and the inevitable social interaction with strangers, new unintroduced players and management. These thoughts and feelings should have been recognised and dealt with, but like all my negative feelings in the past, and in particular those surrounding my speech, they were suppressed deep into my psyche, to fester and mutate to create crippling feelings of self-inadequacy later on.

I attended the next few training sessions with the county seniors at O'Toole Park. There were no revolutionary new drills or exercises to be performed. They employed the standard drills that you would see in any senior club around the country but the intensity was defi-nitely raised and the panel would collectively make fewer mistakes, fewer balls were spilled and the players would let one another know whether their individual and collective standards had dropped. There were distinct groups within the panel and many players would generally stick with their fellow club-mates when away from the playing pitches. I was happy to keep myself to myself. Gavin, by this time, had been experiencing problems with an arthritic knee and he had not been playing for some time. I was on my own and once everything was kept within the confines of polite small talk I was generally happy and content to be part of the panel. For the moment, the negative self-talk was only a silent chatter.

The under-21 Offaly replay was to be played in Parnell Park. This time, my father had read about the impending match in the paper and insisted he was going to come. He sat in the stands as we took to the field, another wet day with the inevitable greasy ball and difficulties with handling the hurley. The first half was a turgid affair, both sides struggling with the conditions. I missed a long-distance free and was generally out of the play for long periods but my man was quiet so, as a back, I had been relatively successful. I was more involved in the second half. I got in a number of clearances and enjoyed the rousing sound of the crowd as it cheered every clearance. But Offaly were too strong all over the field and they found it easier to get scores. Our forwards had to struggle just to obtain primary possession. Offaly cantered home easy winners in the end. I was satisfied with my performance on the day but disappointed that in my final year as an under-21 I had only played a portion of two county games.

I was subsequently asked by the senior county manager to join the extended panel for the first-round Leinster championship match against Wexford in Croke Park. I was not on the list of the substitutes and was really only there to experience the location and occasion; however I was still happy to be involved after the disappointment of the Offaly defeat. It was a great experience to run out with the team, hear the crowd and warm up with them before the match. For long periods of the game we were competing with Wexford in all positions and Seán Power, my former DCU colleague, was hurling very well. Like most superior teams, Wexford hurled better in the second half and pulled away, achieving their first win on the way to ultimately winning the All-Ireland that year.

The only hurling I was involved in subsequent to Dublin's exit from the championship was with my club. Most of my time was spent studying for my finals and thinking about what I was going to do next year. Whatever path I decided to take I knew it was going to be a monumental year for both my career and my ability to deal with discomfort and apprehension because of my stammer.

5

Interview

*A*sk any stammerer what one of their most feared speaking situations would be and invariably a job interview would be in the top three. I would hazard a guess and say that a job/college presentation and maybe giving a wedding speech would also appear on the list. Before the McGuire Programme, I simply had to attend a number of job interviews because my career and my livelihood depended upon it. Despite my best efforts, I simply could not avoid doing job interviews. Verbal communication is obviously an integral part of the whole process and there is an inherent standard required of verbal dexterity and verbosity in order to attain the ultimate prize. At least following the McGuire Programme I was equipped physically and mentally with some tools to control my fear, increase my concentration and deal with feared words or sounds (which always seemed to crop up unannounced when the pressure was on).

Toward the end of 1996, I was nearing the completion of my degree and considering my options. Deep down I wanted to stay and do the Masters and play hurling with DCU for another year, but the general consensus among my classmates was that it was essential for your long-term career to obtain a training contract with one of the Big 6 accounting and auditing firms (located in various elegant offices in the more affluent areas of the city centre). Everyone bought into the process of applying for these firms, irrespective of the personal goals of the individual.

In the mid-90s it was a buyers' market in terms of job applications and those studying Accounting and Finance had to send complex and almost intimately detailed standard application forms to the Big 6 accounting firms operating in the market for the purposes of obtaining a much-coveted three-year training contract. Contracts should have been awarded for simply completing one of these application forms but the process was made more Herculean by the fact that everyone was competing with one another and trying to make theirs the stand-out version amongst the pile. One of the questions asked (on every application form) was whether you suffered from a disability or not. This question concerned me. The question probably could not be asked today in the current politically correct climate but there it was, staring me in the face, right after the question asking me whether I worked well under pressure. I thought about it for a long time and realised that potentially it was a good thing as it allowed me to disclose my stammer before the actual interview (if I got one) and surely that would reduce the pressure on me to speak well. However, what if the question was used as a screening technique and those with (perhaps certain) disabilities would not be entertained and not given a chance at an interview? I discussed my concerns with one of my lecturers and after a few minutes of embarrassing blocks and sounds he finally understood my concerns. His sage response was to include the details of my stammer on three application forms and omit it on the other three. This seemed all perfectly logical and acceptable to me and I selected the three to include the details of my stammer at random (because to me, all six firms would give me the same uniform training contract).

The applications forms were duly completed and sent out and I was confident I had completed them to the best of my ability. I spent the next few weeks waiting expectantly for a letter or email from the respective HR departments. The eventual results were not surprising to me. The three application forms with details of my stammer did not generate a single response while I got called for an interview from the three firms that knew nothing about the impending stuttering interview candidate heading to their firm.

Their only exposure to me was the details of my examination results, my involvement in hurling and my desire to become a chartered accountant. I had perhaps gone a little overboard about hurling in my application forms.

I was satisfied with the three offers of an interview and duly focused on the first scheduled one. Speechwise, I was not feeling good. I never (before the McGuire Programme) believed that I would achieve a comprehensible speaking performance in the confines of an interview room. I had relatively little interview experience as such, but I knew the general theme and construction of one and I knew it did not play to my strengths. At that time, I carried a pen and yellow pocket notebook everywhere I went just in case my speech evaporated altogether under any pressure. This seemed logical and indeed very practical to me at the time and I often congratulated myself on my ingenuity and foresight.

Like any good candidate heading to an interview, I prepared as best as I could, memorising my answers in my original application form, reading up on the firm and trying to anticipate what questions would be put my way. However, I was petrified but hugely realistic at the same time. I knew that I would not be able to communicate (there were no past positive experiences to draw from) and that not only was there fear surrounding speaking but also shame, guilt and self-hate because I was unable to convey what I really wanted to say in an interview situation. All throughout my life, speaking has been a negative experience for me, leaving me emotionally scarred and humiliated. The fear accumulates days before a known scheduled speaking event. This pre-event anxiety is often worse that the actual event itself as the mind sometimes exaggerates and heightens the negative consequences of speaking poorly. There are many facets of the fear experienced: fear of being perceived as incoherent and incompetent, fear of being misunderstood, fear of being judged, and the more general fear of being in an unpleasant and uncomfortable environment and generally suffering stress to my mind and body. In addition, I would experience conflicting heightened emotions of fear, sadness and self-hate that reinforced my life-long-held belief that I would never be able to string two words together when it really counted.

Unfortunately, the body's reaction to fear is flight or fight: pump adrenaline through the body, increase the heart rate and stimulate the muscles. These physical conditions are certainly not conducive to staying calm and breathing evenly, two prerequisites for someone who stammers and who needs to speak well. There is also a huge amount of frustration too surrounding communication, of not being able to properly express knowledge, feelings or opinions verbally.

As I approached the firm's stately offices the afternoon of the interview, in my slightly oversized, newly acquired navy suit (purchased specifically for the trials of the interview process), I continually thought about how painful and humiliating this experience was going to be. I had succeeded somewhat by actually attending the interview but on this occasion my fear of not having some sort of career progression outweighed my desire to avoid the event. I had practiced somewhat, in front of the mirror at home, watching and listening to myself but even then I stammered on my own, utterly convinced my physical speaking mechanisms of throat, vocal chords, tongue and lips were faulty. My best hope was to somehow remain calm, keep my answers as short as possible and hope that the hard-nosed experienced accountants and HR people of the firm would go easy on me and look past my verbal difficulties.

It is a general rule of thumb that receptionists at offices like the Big 6 are young and attractive, always apparently busy and appear slightly annoyed when you have to temerity to interrupt them and notify them of your existence. This particular receptionist was especially busy, fielding calls on an expensive-looking headset and computer combination while simultaneously questioning me with her eyes, why I was in front of her, looking at her. I had planned for such an occasion as this for weeks in advance and duly produced my email confirmation from the left breast pocket of my suit and presented it to her, almost bowing my head, as if to say this is the reason I disrupted her day. She read the email while still conducting a conversation through her headset and nodded her head in the direction of the waiting area, indicating I was to leave her alone and sit down. I congratulated myself on another situation where I had avoided having to say my name, with its double plosive sounds being the most difficult combination of words to say for me personally.

Some time later a genial middle-aged HR lady silently approached me, introduced herself and asked me to follow her to the interview room. It was then that I was suddenly gripped with foreboding and dread; there definitely was no turning back now and no amount of producing emails from my pockets would help me avoid having to speak. At this time of my life, I was totally and utterly convinced that my stammer would destroy my life. Despite my convictions I occasionally somehow mustered the courage or sheer obstinacy to give something like this a try and take my chances. I knew my odds of success were very slim – nothing in my life experiences to date could convince me otherwise – but something inside me always wanted to push, to do battle and not give up. I would have to rely on that spark of determination over the next few years.

The interview room was the standard shape and size of many interview rooms I would have the pleasure to spend time in over the next few years. An oval-shaped dark mahogany table dominated the room, encircled by sturdy modern steel chairs, not designed for comfort. The décor was grey and neutral, complementing the stereotypical personas of accountants. A large house plant stood proudly in the corner, seeming almost out of place in the sterile environment. Some prints of Dublin city and its most famous landmarks adorned the walls. I was directed to sit on one side of the table while the opposite side housed the previously mentioned HR lady, one audit partner (male) and an audit manager (also male), who I was told would take charge of training that year's crop of new employees. I was offered a glass of water, shook my head as my way of declining the offer and lowered myself into the chair, feeling its cold back and handles press against my suit as I waited for the hangman's axe to fall.

At this point my body was supercharged with tension and I was rigid with anxiety. I managed to utter my first yes, no responses without too much of an effort though I did notice my audience staring intently at my opened and gaping mouth during the three-second extended delay when no sounds came out. Eyes narrowed and brows were furrowed in consternation. If I had any doubt about whether my audience had discovered I had a stammer, those doubts evaporated when I tried to respond to the question 'Tell me a little bit about yourself, please.' At this stage, I could hear and feel my heart pounding in my ears. I was starting to perspire heavily as my shirt stuck to my back. My legs started to tremble and my vision blurred. I know I intended to talk about hurling, but I could not enunciate the H sounds, so I regarded the next best alternative as substituting 'hurling' with the word 'football' but the F sound caught me off-guard and that did not work. The S for sport was insurmountable too but I was alright with T's lately, so I managed to convey that I played tennis for the college while they clearly read on the copy of my application laid out before them that I played hurling. Now, I must confess – and I have a clear memory of this looking back now, in retrospect, in the context of speaking well using my tools and techniques currently – that I was entirely and without exception *incomprehensible* for the first few minutes of the interview. However, I was convinced I had covered my tracks with my word substitution and when I was finished what felt like a Shakespearian monologue, I exhaled audibly and gazed expectantly at my audience for the next question. The HR lady pretended to write furiously on my application form the salient points she had garnered from my speech but in reality it was her way of avoiding eye contact with me. The audit partner and manager looked at me with a mixture of incredulity and pity respectively, with the former sliding a glass of water over to me in a display of solicitude I respected him for.

The interview continued in the same vein, with the questions becoming noticeably more succinct with the defined purpose of eliciting the shortest response times as possible. Everyone knew this was a farce – they did and I did – but yet we had all to endure this convention because that is the way that interviews were conducted in those times. The worst was yet to come. The HR lady, evidently excruciatingly uncomfortable with my babbling noises, kindly enquired where I hoped to be in five years. I knew this question was coming up, I was duly prepared but when I opened my mouth, nothing – and I mean nothing – came out. Not a sound, not an outflow of air, just a display of my fillings and missing back teeth. By this time I was drenched in sweat, my shirt clung to my back and front and I was wiping my hands on my trousers in anticipation of the handshake at the end of the interview I knew was coming. I was somehow counting in my head, without intention, counting the period of time my mouth was open and not producing sounds.

Ten, eleven. They just kept staring. Fifteen, sixteen. Their eyes were burning into me. I was exhausted. My heart was beating faster than any occasion in any match or training session I had. I felt dizzy, I felt weak. Just stop. The thought instantly came to me. Just fucking stop.

I felt myself standing up and reaching for my pen and pocket notebook I carried everywhere. I put them on the table. Everyone's eyes drifted to the pen and notebook. They hadn't a clue what was going on. All the while, I was standing to attention, right in front of them, staring blankly at the wall. I felt like fainting. I knew the colour had flushed from my cheeks. I just stood there, doing nothing, everyone slowly turning their eyes up toward me, while my body tried to recalibrate itself for normal functioning. I don't know why I stood up. Perhaps my body wanted to subconsciously protect itself from further trauma and somehow took over the controls for my bodily functions. My vision regained focus and clarity and I slowly sat down, not saying a word, not willing to put myself through any more torture by stammering wildly over the simplest of words.

The audit partner cleared his throat, sipped his water and placed his pen on the table. He recognised how difficult the interview process was for me and he apologised if any of the questions caused me to become uncomfortable. I appreciated his candour. He then explained that accounting was a career with multiple occasions where good verbal communications were necessary and that, with respect, perhaps it was not the career for me. I should, he advised, rethink my long-term career goals.

My brain was not processing any of this at the time. I heard his words clearly but the overriding emotion I had at that time was the desire to leave and leave quickly. The interview concluded, mercifully, hands were shook, sweaty palms and all. I knew this was bad, really bad, and that that was probably the worst speaking situation of my life. Realistically, I had no one else to blame. I had to apportion blame to someone; otherwise the whole process did not make sense. There had to be a culprit for this affliction that had ruined my career before it even got started. I duly blamed myself because my father hadn't been in the room with me causing me to stammer; I hadn't had a row with anyone beforehand upsetting me. It was because I was simply incapable of verbally communicating.

I walked all the way home from the city centre, the sweat drying into my skin. I was relieved that the interview was over and told myself that realistically I needed to do something about my speech. Immediately. Yes, that would be the wake-up call that was needed. That was the catalyst. I would never speak like that again.

Despite my silent promises to myself I did nothing about my speech. My only act was to throw away my remaining two offers for interviews. I did not contact the relevant offices to say I would not be attending. I simply did not show up. I consciously decided not to endure another episode like this last debacle.

Looking back at times like these I often wondered why I didn't immediately look into tackling my problem. I felt alone, isolated, ashamed and bitter, angry that I was cursed with this affliction when everyone else could speak with no problems. Like any addict (and I was one, chronically addicted to avoiding situations and not facing my stammer), I just could not admit to myself I had a problem; I just thought I could spend my life avoiding every situation and get a job somehow, somewhere, in an office where talking was not relevant or necessary. I clung on to these naive expectations despite the over-whelming evidence that was constantly presented to me that I had a serious problem.

Instead, I retreated further into myself, camped myself in the library studying for my finals, and simply hoped for the best.

6

College – Post-Graduate Year

Given my performance in my one serious job interview and my almost instant reaction of throwing away the other two offers of an interview, I determined that, rather unsurprisingly, the best option for my long-term career was actually to do the Masters in Accounting in DCU. I justified the decision to myself by rationally affirming that employers would find the additional letters after my name enormously attractive on a CV and that I was only increasing my chances of securing a job interview. I obviously failed to realise that my problem was not in obtaining an interview, it was my actual performance in one. I ignored that conundrum for the time being. I was busy deluding myself. The fact that I had another year hurling in DCU greatly appealed to me but that was only an added bonus and not the sole determinant in my decision to continue with education. Or so I told myself.

I duly applied for the programme confident in my ability to obtain the requisite grades. I met with the programme head, Professor Pierce, a keen Wexford hurling supporter and someone who was hugely helpful and influential while I did my Masters. We briefly chatted, mostly about hurling but also how the postgraduate course was different to the undergraduate one and he promised me I would find it very enjoyable.

The week or two of final exams came and went without too much incident. There was the usual level of apprehension and tension but I had prepared myself throughout the year (I just didn't have to capacity to cram and achieve successful grades like other students did). I had done so many exams at that stage that I knew, approximately, the grade I would get when an examination was over. There were no exam surprises, nothing came up in any of the papers that I had not revised or was not familiar with, being especially diligent completing past exam papers leading up my finals. I was satisfied I had done my best, worked hard and was going to be successful with my application to do the Masters.

Another summer was passed in Percy Place with AIB Investment Managers. My duties did not evolve from the previous summers of shredding, binding and filing, but I was content to linger in my comfort zones. I knew most of the people there, got on well with everyone and enjoyed the morning and afternoon cycle to and from work. I would spend the evenings playing hurling and football with my club, trying to stay away from my father and only face my fear of speaking when I simply could not avoid the situation. All the while I was avoiding speaking situations; I was building up my emotional charge surrounding my feared words and sounds. I was ignorant of the fact that such avoidance behaviours would have future crippling effects on my speech.

I was never under the impression that AIB would approach me on my last day of work and present me with a lucrative and enticing contract to join their ranks. I was entirely content with the fact that the summer work looked good on my emaciated CV. I had no other expectations at that time. In retrospect, perhaps, I could have been more forceful and assertive and actively indictated that I was looking for a position after my degree course had finished but no one had approached me about it anyway. I took that as a sign that AIB had other candidates in mind for employment opportunities with them that year.

My year as a Masters student was my most enjoyable one in DCU. Around thirty of us were doing the Masters, mostly from my Accounting and Finance class but there were some from other universities who has transferred specifically because of the quality of the course and the lecturing staff. I was aware from the start of the year that I would have to perform an oral presentation in front of the class at the end of the term and this pre-event anxiety occupied my thoughts for many months. I thought about avoiding, about being absent that day or about simply informing the lecturer that I couldn't do the presentation. However, the presentation was to be a joint one; I was to share the stage with a class colleague and our respective grades would be dependent on a collective result. If I avoided I jeopardised my classmate's grade along with my own. This time my cowardice would have direct consequences and I rattled my brain for months trying to come up with a solution. I put it aside, dismissing it as something that would somehow magically resolve itself as time moved on and decided to deal with it at a later date.

Despite my anxiety, the traditional lectures were more relaxed and focused than the undergraduate ones and I thoroughly enjoyed all the classes and the related subject matter. I never experienced any pre-event tension going into classes because none of the lecturers on the programme actively called on unsuspecting students to participate; it was not their teaching style. In any event the volume of the material was so dense that there was no time for waiting for embarrassed students to formulate answers. The lectures clipped on at a satisfyingly steady pace.

Once again I was in the familiar routine of library and hurling. When the college hurling season started I was selected to be captain. This honour is usually bestowed on a final-year student but this year there were a number of worthy candidates to choose from. I was delighted with my selection but also worried about any speeches or verbal communication I would have to undertake in that role. It was one thing talking to the lads in the dressing room before and after a match. It was another thing entirely to have to be an orator and have to speak well for a formal occasion.

Despite being captain, I was determined not to have to do much talking. Instead I resolved to lead by example and simply play better than I had ever previously done. That year I was a frequent attendee at the DCU gym and on days when there was no formal training I organised lunch-time sessions with some of the available lads so that I had a hurley in my hand every day. The team was shaping up very nicely. We were strong up the centre with Seán Óg and Johnny Sheehan, but we also had skilful wing-backs in Paddy Murphy and Dermot Beirne. We had a favourable draw for the Fitzgibbon Cup that year which meant we only had to beat Jordanstown (a Northern Ireland university) and we would be attending the semi-final weekend, which was going to be held in University College Cork.

Training intensity was ramped up and Danny McGovern was determined that we would be fully ready for the forthcoming season. We had a mixed league campaign that year but in reality all our attention was focused on the Fitzgibbon Cup; we desperately wanted to become the first DCU side to reach the Fitzgibbon Cup semi-finals.

I still avoided home wherever possible. My interaction with my family was intentionally limited as I knew that I could not endure many more episodes with my father. I had recognised the correlation between the tension at home and the quality of my speech and I knew that if I was to at least maintain some semblance of fluency with the lads I would have to be out of the house as much as I could. I did not have any relationship with my father. We only saw each other briefly by design. I was acting selfishly for self-preservation purposes and perhaps should have confronted my personal issues with him. However, when I saw glimpses of his temper I knew I had chosen the correct course of action and following an argument I would inevitably spend the next few days in the library or away at matches just to put some distance between myself and the tension-riddled house.

The match against Jordanstown was held in the neutral UCD grounds on another wintry day, but at least this time it was dry. I remember it being a tight match until Johnny Sheehan caught a couple of puck-outs and sent them directly over the bar. I cursed myself for missing an easy free at one stage but I emptied the tank on the field that day and when the match ended I was satisfied with the result and my personal performance. The celebrations continued in the UCD bar after the match and subsequently carried on across the city at DCU later that night. It was shaping up to be the perfect year, and I was determined to spend the remainder of the time to the weekend in Cork preparing for the biggest match of my career.

I began to worry about my career after college. Increasingly, my classmates were receiving good job offers and I was receiving curt replies thanking me for my application and promising to keep my records on file for future (possible) reference. Since the debacle of my last big interview, I tended to focus now on the smaller accounting firms, who I was sure were not inundated with applications from Accounting and Finance graduates from DCU and in all probability would have a less exacting application and interview criteria than the Big 6 firms. However, even during the limited number of small firm interviews I attended I was met with further cold, harsh advice. On every occasion my speech let me down, despite my knowledge, academic grades and apparently well-rounded personality (if you concentrated all our attention on my CV). Every failure reaffirmed in my mind that I simply could not navigate interviews and soon I was running out of potential firms to work for within a reasonable distance to where I lived.

I was beginning to get desperate. It was clear that my speaking performance in interviews was destroying my chances of getting a job. More worryingly, I felt that even if I somehow magically got a job then I could not retain one due to the poor quality of my speech. I was terrified of not having a professional career or future. The pressure to perform at interviews inevitably impinged upon my already crumbling speech and I was locked into this vicious cycle with no obvious solution.

Once again, I focused on hurling, avoiding the painful reality of actually having to confront my stammer. DCU had been drawn against UCC in the semi-finals. They always had an especially strong team, but this year it was stellar. The team contained such future luminaries as Joe Deane and Seánie McGrath (future Cork All-Ireland winners) as well as current Cork senior panellists and under-age intercounty stars.

Our preliminary success in reaching the semi-final weekend brought us closer together as a panel. I got to know a lot more of the guys outside of my immediate circle of friends and I felt that I could call every single one of the players on the panel my friend. Training was intense and dogged. Sometimes tension spilled out and there would be the odd loose stroke but as the captain I took it as a good sign that the team were ready for battle. We bonded in the bar as a group and in the extended bunch of girlfriends, friends and well-wishers my stammering virtually evaporated in the atmosphere of camaraderie, alcohol and hurling.

As expected, UCC were a formidable outfit and despite our aspirations put us to the sword early on. They were more experienced and penetrated our defence at will. Even Seán Óg said after the match that they had played exceptionally well. He was well-acquainted with nearly all their players, having hurled underage for Cork with them. We were all chasing our tails and despite giving our best efforts we were undone by a superior outfit. I was crestfallen. My very last DCU match would go down in defeat. I sought out the company of the manager, Danny McGovern, and stammered an apology for not winning and not playing well. I remember standing beside the pitch, sweaty and dirty from the match, trying to sustain eye contact with my manager. He shook his head, smiled and said that we had both gone out at the very top. It was to be his last match managing the DCU team.

We drowned our sorrows in the Washington Inn bar in Cork city, where the music was pumping and the drink flowed easily. Some former DCU teammates who had been on the team with me in first and second year had made their way down to see the match and share in the atmosphere. That, to me, was what DCU hurling was all about. Lifelong friends, sharing stories and memories of games won and lost.

My performance with DCU contributed to my inclusion on the county panel for 1997. There had been an influx of new players onto the 1996 panel and a new manager in Michael O'Grady. He was a Limerick man and was principally hired to bring some structure and much-needed success to the county set-up. The training was a lot harder than under the previous administration, though it was a lot less enjoyable. From the start, I was not comfortable with the new manager. I felt he did not make enough of an effort to get to know the players on the fringes of the panel. However, despite my uneasiness I was selected to play for many of the early season games, principally because many of the players from O'Toole's (the then Dublin club hurling champions) were absent from the panel, focusing on the Leinster Club Championship competition. I especially recall games against Antrim in Parnell Park, which we won easily, and a tough away encounter against a Paul Flynn-inspired Waterford team. The initial magical feelings of pulling a Dublin jersey over my head always remained but every successive match I played I let my emotions and endemic nervousness and pessimism get the better of me.

It was an entirely different atmosphere to playing with the club or DCU. Again, I was the only player from my club on the panel and that made it difficult with someone with my level of shyness and my stutter to fully integrate with other members of the panel. I remember I always felt pressurised and was always aware of the consequences of not playing well. I deeply missed hurling for the college, the organised events after matches and the sense of community and friendship that inevitably followed. My hurling improved in these conditions but appeared to wilt when I was in the county environment. I should have discussed my issues with the management and perhaps some of the other, more experienced, players and tried to come up with a solution to allow me to play like I played in DCU and with the club. I felt at the time I was not playing to my potential and the management were right in not having me as a regular on the team.

I was an unused sub for some of the National League games and only saw limited game time for the remainder of the year. I was not hurling well enough for inclusion on the first team and I was precariously close to being dropped from the panel. I did not make the championship panel that year and was told to continue to hurl away and train with my club and wait for the call to join the panel next year. I was not holding my breath. I had lost that sense of pure enjoyment I had when I was a kid, striking the ball off the carpark wall. When I had finished hurling with the college my enthusiasm for the sport dipped. There was no longer this sense of overriding freedom or pleasure from training or playing. The training sessions with the county were actively monitored – someone was always looking at and judging you – and the drive I had previously embedded in me to prove to others that I was not just a stutterer had vanished. I just wanted to get training over, not to make too many mistakes and hang around the panel for as long as I could in the hope of becoming a regular first team starter. It was never going to work out that way for me.

In the championship that year, Dublin would win an opening round match against Westmeath. I was not involved. The reward for that win was facing Kilkenny in Croke Park. DJ Carey got about 1-8 that day and Dublin were beaten but the closest I got to proceedings was from my couch, looking at the highlights on TV that night. I definitely would not have made any sort of contribution to the panel if I had been involved. Mentally I was not confident enough in my own ability and experience to develop into a first team player and despite showing fleeting glimpses in early season matches and some training sessions of what I could do I was correctly confined to being a peripheral figure on the panel.

When competitive hurling finished, I was forced to turn my attention to university, and more precisely the impending disaster that was my presentation.

The presentation was about Charles Thomas Horngren, a renowned accounting academic. My colleague, to his credit, agreed to do the presentation with me months back, but I think as the due date got closer he realised we were not going to achieve a stellar grade. I spoke to the professor beforehand and I was so nervous about the presentation I calmly informed him that I would have to do the presentation 'with a few drinks on me'. I think he genuinely thought I was joking. I was going to rely on my induced loquaciousness that limited alcoholic intake generated.

The presentation was on a Wednesday morning but I was in the college bar at 9am drinking bottles of Miller. I had three and felt I could muddle through the presentation. I actually cannot remember one single detail from the event itself. However, I must have appeared nervous and I must have struggled. When I completed my section, one of my good friends applauded, followed slowly by the rest of the class. I was the only presenter to be applauded. Some gestures like that I will never forget. I think I shed a tear or two sitting in my seat watching the next presenter. We must have been awarded a reasonable grade as we both passed that module that semester but I think it was because of the strength of my colleague's presenting skills rather than my own.

I was nearing the end of my Masters and without the enjoyment and security that college hurling gave me my speech was at absolute rock bottom. All my classmates had received offers from a good variety of employers. My marks and exam results were very good but I know that my stammer was destroying any prospects I had. I was absolutely dreading every day simply because someone somewhere would approach me, ask me the time or directions or in some context my name and then I would be revealed as the failure I was.

Fortunately, DCU Business School at that time offered two chartered accountants' training contracts, working in the administration section of the business school. The position principally involved administration but also dealing with purchasing and the main finance department. In truth, the exposure to accounting and finance was very limited. I was talking to Professor Pierce one afternoon in his cramped and cluttered office and he broached the subject of my failure to attain a training contract with an accounting firm following the completion of my Masters. I muttered half-excuses about being busy hurling and focusing all my attention on my exams but I am sure he knew my failure was due to my problems with my stammer in an interview setting. He discussed the position with me, elaborating a little on what it would entail, but crucially it would allow me to train as a chartered accountant, complete my final accountancy exams and become a qualified chartered accountant. He reassured me that there would be no interview; he was confident I was a suitable fit for the position and without hesitation I eagerly accepted the offer. In all honestly that was my last chance; if I was not offered that position I would have never worked as an accountant.

I had earned a degree and Masters from DCU and was ready to begin my accountancy career. I had achieved these through hard work and dogged determination and was proud of myself, given my difficulties at home and my stutter. Although I had not obtained a lofty training contract in a top accounting firm like many of my peers, I felt well on my way to being able to move out of the family home and begin my new life. I was simultaneously terrified about starting my new job, having to introduce myself to new people and having to achieve a basic level of fluency in order to function as a trainee accountant.

It was time to do what my father had wanted me to do for a long time – face the real world.

7

Training Contract

The difficulty with trying to remember what I was like at 21 or 22 is that it is very difficult to put myself back into the mindset of an out-of-control stammerer.

Physically, I was fit and healthy; my headaches, although occurring occasionally, did not affect my life to any great degree and when they did come they could be treated by over-the-counter medication.

My mental state, however, was very fragile and is difficult for me to revisit.

When I say I was an out-of-control stammerer I mean that the dominant thoughts in my psyche for the majority of the day and night were about stammering, the effects of stammering, potential future occasions when I know I would stammer and trying to devise schemes to avoid stammering (and therefore speaking) whenever I could. Most 21-year-olds would have been thinking about a possible year abroad, their first tentative steps into employment, relationships and generally having a good time. Mine were enslaved by my stutter and my stubborn refusal to do anything about it. I was absolutely, rigidly convinced that there was nothing I could do in order to speak well on the occasions when, for example, I had to answer a phone call, confront someone in authority or express my emotions. My fleeting sense of fluency in college had been eroded.

I could not maintain my feelings of self-confidence and acceptance since I was removed from that supportive environment. I did not have the mental strength and emotional intelligence to prepare for new chapters in my life. I was always forecasting, always predicting what future speaking occasions I would have, and in every single one of them I would fail miserably. This was because my track history in speaking well when I had to had been consistently miserable. Stammering was something that in my mind had been thrust upon me by God (why me, God?) and I was burdened with it for the rest of my life. I did not want to think like this forever. It was not fair. I felt victimised. There was no one in my life to challenge such negative beliefs. No one who could tell me to look at the positives in my life – see how far I had come in life even with this cursed disability. I did not have the knowledge or bravery to challenge these beliefs that were revolving around inside my head, all day every day.

When I began work as a trainee accountant in DCU there were no occasional glimpses of fluency with the lads. No college hurling matches to boost my confidence and no more nights in the bar trying to get to know someone I fancied. Every working day I was confronted with something new: someone new to talk to; some task to complete which required some verbal interaction; different stresses and pressures. I was experiencing new challenges both verbal and non-verbal every day and I was constantly being confronted with obstacles that I had to deal with on a psychological level.

Working as a trainee accountant in DCU forced me to seriously confront my stammering mentality for the first time. I could not avoid speaking situations in work and I definitely could not substitute feared words or sounds with a suitable alternative I could articulate. I think the pressure of work and of not knowing what speaking challenges were going to be presented to me every day triggered a deterioration in my stammer and overall negativity.

I wanted to have a successful career and attempted to rationalise all negative feelings associated with my speech and my mindset at that time. Due to the strained relationships with my family I knew that I could not confide in them or ask for help, or just say 'You know what, I'm at a really low point, I don't know what to do, I just need somewhere to lay low for a bit, gather my thoughts and go again.'

I did not earn enough money during my training contract to be able to move out of the family home. Around this time my father's acerbic comments in an argument would centre on my earning prowess and his desired wish that I move out of home because I was obviously unhappy there. He automatically equated working with earning a sufficient wage to live independently. Despite my protestations, he was convinced I should have been long gone from the house. His only point of reference was the relationship between his father and himself and how at 21 he had moved to another country, gained meaningful employment and was well on the way to becoming a father. In his eyes, I was somewhat lagging behind. I was still at home, enjoying my mother's cooking and having her wash my dirty hurling gear about fifty times a week. Tensions in the house inevitably rose and my preferred method of dealing with any conflict at this stage bore an uncanny resemblance to how I dealt with my stutter. I pretended everything was alright, avoided interactions whenever I could and sought solace in long walks sustained by my Walkman.

Aside from stammering, I was exhibiting some ... interesting ... mental behaviours too. I would have wild, almost manic, mood swings that would appear, disappear and reappear, seemingly at random. Thoughts of prior poor speaking occasions would reduce me to tears. The status of my relationship with my father would be deeply unsettling, dominating my thoughts for a few minutes and preventing me from undertaking any other tasks. There would be a physical lump in my throat and pain across my chest when I thought about the arguments we had and the comments that were directed at me.

I also carried an oppressive sense of emptiness inside me. I did not know who I really was. I did not like the stuttering person I saw in the mirror and who also flinched when confronted with his stuttering mentality. The stammer *always* won. Darren Benham always backed down. I considered myself a coward.

I tried to focus on the positives in my life: I was just starting my accounting career, I was hurling at a reasonable level, I was fit, I had a degree and a Masters and yet something was pulling me further into myself, dulling all of my achievements and destroying any chance I had of pulling myself out of the abyss just long enough to do something about my speech.

I also had a very unclear self-image. I didn't know who I was. I later rationalised this was because of my contrasting successes when speaking amongst the lads as opposed to the uniform failures I had speaking in the real world. Which representation was the real me? I didn't know if I was naturally shy or a repressed extrovert. Sometimes I would be elated, over a hurling performance or hearing my favourite song on the Walkman, then two minutes later manically depressed when I thought about having to return home or due to the shame I felt when having to point at the menu in McDonalds.

I felt quite clearly as this stage that there was a finite limit to the emotional and mental trauma I could endure. I knew that, eventually, along the way I could break if I continued to deal with the issues in my life in the manner I was currently handling them. I was not mature enough to realise that I needed, at least, some external support and in all likelihood professional help. I thought everybody felt like this. My only perspective in life came from someone with a chronic stutter and having my thoughts consumed by stuttering and, by corollary, embarrassment, unhappiness, anxiety, shame and so on were the default positions. I just felt burdened with these thoughts and emotions, never knowing at the time that there was something wrong in feeling like this, that I actually wasn't supposed to be having thoughts like this at that age. When I recognised I was having these feelings I rationalised that they were normal, that everyone had these thoughts trying to figure out who they were and that no one had a clear view of the path they would take in life at 21 or 22. But with me, it was more than that. The burden seemed heavier and more oppressive or, at least for me, my skills at dealing with the daily stresses of life were clearly not as developed at everyone else's.

I just tried to manage each day as best as I could. There was another graduate who had been awarded a training contract – John Kilcoyne – and for three years we shared an office and the associated respective duties and responsibilities. John did not do the Masters but he had completed my undergraduate course. He was friendly and smart, originated from Mayo and was living near campus. Our main function was administrative support to the lecturers and teaching staff of the business school as well as being their intermediary with the main finance department. That meant we would handle the lecturers' requests for funds, payment for their exam scripts and other related administrative duties. Our duties also involved processing corrected exam scripts and inputting the physical results into the main university computer system that gathered and correlated all the results. The system would them spit out the results which the respective lecturers would review and discuss individually and collectively and ultimately agree on the students' grades. This system was interesting and revealing the first time but over the course of three years I grew to hate having to spend endless hours inputting and processing data. It certainly was of no practical benefit to me as a trainee chartered accountant. All my contemporaries would be undertaking very specific and practical tasks in their training contracts while I was processing exam results.

Although my financial duties were limited during my training contract, we were never under pressure and working hard was unheard of. It also meant that we could spend additional time studying during the day and completing assignments when the evening professional examination lectures began. The professional examination syllabus was run by the Institute of Chartered Accountants and lectures were held over some weekends and mid-week for a few months every year. Although we were disadvantaged by the lack of practical work experience in DCU, we were fresh and able to concentrate at lectures. Other less fortunates would be highly pressurised during the day and they would slump on their desks and inevitably fall asleep while I was diligently taking notes, getting ready for the impending exams.

The job also required a lot of interaction with my former lecturers. The relationships seemed strange and awkward at first but they were uniformly friendly and would politely knock on our office door, shyly asking us for our assistance if that was alright with us. I developed an interest in the academic world and was fascinated how the lecturers built a career from continuously learning, researching, publishing and teaching. I would try to ask many of them how they got a job as a lecturer, how hard was it to become a doctor or professor of something, while trying to assess whether I would have the capabilities to sustain a career as an accounting academic.

The obvious problem was that any career in academia would involve teaching, lecturing or giving tutorials and at that time this was simply insurmountable to me. Nothing in my life up to that point had shown me that I was capable of going into a room full of strangers and imparting my knowledge to them. I put myself into the position of the expectant student, sitting in front of a lecturer unable to say fundamental accounting words like 'debit' or 'credit' or 'liabilities'. I wouldn't be too happy as a student to have to endure a lecturer who could not speak. I quickly resigned myself to the fact that I would never be an academic.

My colleagues in work adapted their behaviours around me. Whenever I spoke it was obvious I stammered and that I was uncomfortable with verbal communication. I would avoid eye contact, and I would blush and withdraw inside myself. My colleagues became aware of my sensitivities and therefore they would interact with me through email rather than in person or through the phone. John would do most of the talking in the meetings we had with the other administrative staff. Everyone just fell into roles to accommodate me and, while I was grateful at the time, I was embarrassed and ashamed that people had to change their behaviour and think of my emotions before confronting me with a work issue. Older administrative staff who had historically steered cleared of email and the internet suddenly became expert at sending me one-line requests through the college intranet.

When the county team reconvened for training at the end of the year, I was not looking forward to the season ahead. I had been playing with the club but both our football and hurling senior teams were losing most of their games. Both panels contained players who were well over thirty and there was not the constant influx of new players that every successful team needs. Attendances at training were poor, attitudes were worse and morale was low. While working in DCU I could still arrange to go hurling with some of the college lads at lunchtime and these sessions were of a higher standard that the collective training sessions I had with the club. The DCU guys would tell me how the college team was getting on, who was playing well and what the new manager was like. I missed those collective sessions and the college matches, but especially the self-made entertainment in the bar.

I played a number of friendly and competitive matches for the county team in the early part of the new year. I had not greatly progressed since the previous years. I was effectively playing at a lower level now as my club team had been demoted to intermediate hurling and football and most of the training I was doing was on my own and informally with the lads in DCU. I could not officially play for DCU as I was an employee and not a student so I tried to organise as many unofficial sessions with the lads as I could. There was no guidance from the county set-up either regarding my performances and progression. The management seemed to just be waiting until the starting players from the previous year returned from playing with their clubs. Many of them were still involved with the Dublin and Leinster club championships and were therefore absent from the early season training sessions with the county. I was not enjoying the training or matches and my performances consequently dipped. I remember a friendly against Tipperary where I was run ragged and exposed in the corner-back position. I was marking a new kid on the block, Liam Cahill. However, in that position you need some cover and assistance from the half-backs and midfield. The whole team performed badly but I remember thinking to myself that the corner-backs would solely be blamed. Sure enough, the full back line got a roasting at training the next day. Liam Cahill eventually ended up winning an All-Star that year and I like to think I contributed to his early career successes by playing so poorly that day.

I didn't feel the same sense of unity as I did on the DCU team. The self-belief and confidence needed to overcome negative beliefs and perceptions were just not there. I resigned myself to just doing the best I could and hoping that something magically would turn my fortunes around and that I would rediscover the form that had first brought me onto the panel.

That summer I was glad I did not make the county championship team. Dublin were drawn against Kilkenny and were duly hammered, destroyed by a much superior team. I remember DJ Carey ran riot. The management came in for a bit of criticism from the media and instigated changes to the panel. A couple of months after the defeat to Kilkenny the manager phoned me at home to tell me that I would not be asked to re-join the panel for the subsequent hurling year. I cannot say it was unexpected. My hurling had not developed since first joining the senior panel in 1996. I had not gotten any fitter, stronger or more skilful. I was now playing at a lower level with my club and that affected my performances. I had not mixed in with the other members of the panel, I did not feel comfortable at training and felt the huge time commitment involved, travelling to and from matches, was not worth it given the very limited time I was given wearing a jersey. In fairness, I had no one to blame but myself. I tried to focus on other aspects of my life and convinced myself that I was still young enough to prove myself again to the next management team in charge of the county setup. I filed another disappointment in my life into the recesses of my psyche.

I did not discuss being dropped from the panel with my family. In many ways I was disappointed but knew there were better players currently playing better hurling in Dublin in my position than me. It was something I had to put behind me. I had lost most of the joy and enjoyment I obtained from playing simply because of the pressures involved with playing for the county, the defeats, the poor perfor- mances and the time spent on buses and coaches trying to avoid conversations with teammates I had trouble bonding with.

Around this time too, I met my ex-wife. She and a couple of my club teammates were attending a party for one of their friends in town. I had met the lads walking towards their destination as I was making the solitary journey home from the city centre. They insisted I join them despite my weak protestations and after some negotia- tions I was on my way. I rationalised that it would keep me out of the house for a couple of hours. In the pub I located a quiet corner and scanned everyone in the room, trying to determine whether I would have to speak to anyone that night. Eventually I was introduced to a tall, brown-haired girl who was friends with my teammates and, using every bit of small talk I could muster, we started to get to know each other. That was the start of our relationship.

I was also studying long hours in preparation for my final profes- sional examinations to become a chartered accountant. I was confident going in that I had prepared as best as I could and now it was only a matter of refining my technique, practicing some prior exam questions and getting my timing right.

At the time the results came out I was working as a trainee chartered accountant in a well-known medium-sized practice on

Northumberland Road. The powers that be at DCU recognised that some sort of actual practical accounting experience would be useful for us two trainee chartered accountants and so each of us were seconded to this firm for six months. The managing partner had close ties with one of the primary lecturers on the programme and the arrangement apparently suited both organisations.

For six months I fielded technical questions and queries from the other accountants. I was technically very good but had no hands-on practical experience. This lack of experience was continually queried by one of the partners I had to work with and he simply could not comprehend how I could not undertake even the most basic accounting tasks without direct supervision but could recite the exact accounting standards to deal with hedging and financial instruments.

On the morning the results were published I headed to the offices of the Institute of Chartered Accountants Ireland on Pembroke Road. The results were displayed on cork noticeboards in a room just off the reception area. My heart was pounding as I located my ID number and, adjusting my gaze, duly discovered that I had passed.

I had attained a huge milestone in my life, effectively reaching the end of my academic journey. Indeed the examinations themselves were called the FAEs (Final Admitting Examinations) but the students colloquially called them 'Fuck All Else'.

I started to feel like a grown-up. I was nearing the end of my training contract in DCU and I could now start to look to the future.

The only problem with finishing my contract was that I would have to get another job and that obviously entailed having to undertake job interviews. This time there would not be the safety net of a contract offered by DCU. I simply *had* to perform well at these interviews in order to secure employment and start my life away from home.

8

Speech Therapy

At the end of my last working day in DCU, I left early, locked the door and dropped the office door key in my supervisor's post-box. At this time, John was working in Northumberland Road during his secondment term and for the previous few weeks I had lived a solitary existence in our little shared office, left alone with my thoughts about the impending end of my training contract. I knew I was hopelessly ill-prepared for 'proper' accounting work with my limited practical experience but I also recognised that my speech and mentality were at an all-time low. My early departure on the last day was a predetermined attempt to avoid any contact with my fellow employees who had patiently and diligently worked with me for the last three-and-a-half years. I simply could not face anyone. I was disgusted by my own cowardice and my unwillingness to mark the occasion of the completion of my training contract. I wanted to just run away.

I was terrified about the impending job interview process. I planned to use the services of a recruitment agency in order to centralise the job hunting process (and minimise the necessity for actual job interviews) and I cowardly promised myself that I would accept the first offer of a job. Despite my antagonistic attitude towards God, I felt he would good-naturedly ensure that the first job offer I received would not only be ideal but a comfortable life-long fit.

I sent off my truncated CV to a small number of recruitment agencies specialising in dealing with newly qualified chartered accountants and was encouraged by the responses I got (needless to say, I had learned a harsh lesson during my university years and made no reference to my stammer in my CV or covering letters).

I mumbled and stumbled my way though one interview with a well-known recruitment agency and they asked whether I would be interested in interviewing for a position as the financial accountant in a manufacturing firm in Santry, Dublin. A couple of days later I nervously made my way to the factory in my slightly oversized suit, knowing almost nothing about the factory and inwardly praying that the interviewer would somehow do all the talking and be entirely satisfied with yes and no answers. The interviewer was a young financial controller working with a related company but responsible for the hiring of all accounting staff. He was relaxed and gloriously garrulous, diverting the conversation on many occasions to hurling, then soccer, then his own social life, how his own career was progressing and other irrelevant details that ensured my own talking time would be gratefully limited.

I somehow manged to keep my speech and anxiety in the realm of comprehension for the duration of the interview. I could tell by the direction the interview questions were going that in all proba-bility I would be offered the job. I was asked what salary I expected and because I could not say twenty, I substituted £19,000 for £25,000 simply because I had less trouble with N sounds. It effectively was worth £6,000 a year to me to stutter for less time on 'nineteen' than 'twenty'. That was how much I hated stuttering in front of people.

I was offered the job and gratefully accepted it, satisfied with achieving my short-term goal of terminating the job-hunting and interview process. In hindsight, which we all know is a wonderful thing, I should have researched the role more and reflected on my lack of practical experience instead of leaping right in, in order to save myself from additional trauma. I should have definitely asked for more money.

In any event, I was satisfied that with careful budgeting and the continuation of my frugal lifestyle I would very shortly be in a position to rent some place near work and finally make the necessary move from home that I felt would improve my mental health.

The job was pressurised and afforded me much more unwanted responsibility. I was effectively the financial controller of a small manufacturing firm and was responsible for all areas of the finance and accounting functions, from sales invoicing to banking and to the operation of the payroll function. I had no practical experience whatsoever. I knew, *in theory*, how to perform these tasks but it was another matter entirely to complete them correctly in practice. I made mistakes. A lot of them. I was shouted at. I was embarrassed. I was ashamed. This time not just because of my speech but because of my incompetence and inability to master relatively mundane tasks fast enough. I had no support from any other colleagues; I was there at my desk, effectively sinking without a trace and there seemed to be nothing I could do about it. I just thought about surviving each day, getting through it and I believed that eventually things would fall into place.

Despite my lost £6,000 a year I began to earn enough money to move out of the family home, into a small flat on Griffith Avenue, Dublin. I had found the flat with the assistance of a local letting agent and spent one frenzied weekend moving my books, sports gear and other personal belongings from Portland Row to Griffith Avenue. Despite the excitement of moving out I quickly had to deal with the reality of cooking and washing for myself as well as dealing with the unexpected loneliness, which I thought would never have affected me. I enjoyed my own company but it was a different story waking up and rolling off the mattress on the floor in the morning without a solitary sound. I would not say that I missed my family but I missed my sisters and their solidarity. I missed the noise they made in the mornings getting ready and missed our small talk as we passed each other on the way out of the house and the knowing looks we shared when my father raised his voice.

An oppressive blanket of depression enveloped me. This was not how I was supposed to be feeling. I was liberated from home but there were so many other issues in my life that I was unable to control. I was depressed at work. I was not performing to the best of my ability and I was putting in long hours just to justify my salary to the owners. I was still hurling with the club but attendances at training were poor, we were losing games and I put huge pressure on myself to perform to the high standards I knew I could achieve. When I made a mistake or played poorly I would end up analysing the match, going through all the moments when I had effectively failed and reprimanded myself for my incompetence. Sometimes I would starve myself or go running after a match just to punish myself, punish my body for its inability to put in a good match performance.

Every night I dreaded the thought of work and making another error that would result in another comment from the boss, a shake of his head and a look that expressed his frustration at the quantum of my salary and the lack of results he was getting.

Needless to say, with such a bleak emotional outlook, my speech was at rock bottom. I had to email co-workers in the same room in order to communicate with them. I did not have the ability to simply stand up, walk over to them, look them in the eye and converse. I could not look anyone in the eye at this time. At the end of the first financial quarter I was supposed to have prepared a set of up-to-date management accounts for the directors to review and assess the financial performance of the company to date. I spent four consecutive nights working until 1 a.m., gathering all the information and presenting it in a manner that I hoped they would understand and derive benefit from. The pressure was relentless but I was determined that the figures I would have to present at the forthcoming board meeting would be correct and a reflection of the improvement in my own personal working standards and capabilities over the previous couple of months. On the morning of the meeting, I prepared all the relevant documentation and felt ready to present it to the directors in preparation for their meeting. However, I was quickly informed that I would have to give an oral presentation to the directors and explain key changes, figures and increments on the past quarter. I had presumed that my sole responsibility was to produce the figures and present them to the directors to digest themselves. I dragged myself into the meeting, absolutely certain that this was going to be a disaster. The managing director gruffly started the meeting and announced that I would be dealing with the financial statements and that any questions should be directed at me. All through those introductory minutes perspiration dripped from my forehead and brows onto my copy of the financial material that I had to present. My vision blurred and I felt I was going to lose consciousness.

The managing director eventually signalled to me that it was my turn to speak. I opened the first page of the financial material, desperately hoping that the words 'please turn to page 1 of your pack' would be articulated by my strangled vocal chords. But no words came. No air flowed. My lungs froze. My heart stopped beating. My audience was confronted with my gaping mouth, increasingly purple face and the noise of my fist thumping my thigh in a futile attempt to kick-start my speaking process. I was fortunate in that the individual who conducted my job interview was attending the board meeting and after a harrowing silence of three long minutes he took charge of presenting the figures while I stared at the table for the next hour. I remember not being able to look anyone in the eyes for the next few days as my speech and my self-esteem continued to disintegrate.

I bought a bottle of whiskey one day and placed it on the shelves of my sparse kitchen. Despite my attempts in college, I am absolutely not a drinker but every time I went past the kitchen I would take a swig and try to punish myself, to punish my body. I savoured the burning sensation as the fluid went down my throat, knowing it was doing damage to my body. Serves you right, I thought. I hated myself to such a degree that I would try to starve myself for a day, then two days, then a few days at a time just to see the effect on my body. My mindset was thoroughly negative, nothing positive; I was in a vicious circle of avoidance and fear and I could not see any way out. I literally could not open my mouth without choking out sounds.

I felt I could not confide in anyone at the time and I had run out of motivation and determination to carry on. I had started to formulate strategies about how to survive without speaking for my entire life. My whole outlook was completely negative and defeatist. I needed to talk to someone. I remember telling myself to share my thoughts and feelings with my girlfriend because she always gave an objective viewpoint and she never countenanced bullshit.

I remember trying to talk to her about some of these issues and why I was behaving like I was when I just broke down. I remember thinking to myself, so this is what a nervous breakdown is. Nothing mattered to me. I was either going to confide in her or I was not seeing the next day. She had already looked into adult stammering courses (during the times when I showed some glimpses of interest in participating in any form of speech therapy) and recommended someone to me. I knew I had to do something. My social skills were very poor due to my avoidance behaviours all through my life and I was still very much scarred, emotionally and mentally, from the relationships with my family and my stammering. The next steps really needed to work.

There are not many speech therapists working with adult stammerers. It appears to be a rather specialist area; most therapists seem to be involved in working with and assisting stroke victims and other individuals who have lost their speech capabilities. I was rather surprised that there was one speech therapist specialising in adult stammering in Clontarf. I think she was only beginning to build up her practice. At that time she only conducted group sessions. However to initially gain a control reading or level, she conducted an individual interview session with me and video-recorded the process. The interview consisted of a number of personal questions and my reasons for considering the therapy. I remember I attended the session after work, appearing in my shirt and tie having spent the entire day at work predicting another painful speaking experience. I pushed through so many blocks that I ended the session with an unmerciful headache. So much adrenaline had rushed through my body in those minutes that I had to prise my own fingers off the armrests of the chair. My shirt was drenched in sweat. The therapist confided that I had one of the most severe stammers she had experienced. She allowed me to see the recorded version of my interview and it was as if I was looking at somebody with severe mental trauma. My head and torso heaved sideways with every attempt to produce air and not one coherent word could be heard. I drove home genuinely not knowing how I was going to get through life speaking this way, and washed down eight paracetamol with a can of coke for my headache, feeling utterly isolated and inconsolable.

The group sessions began a week later. I remember sitting in a large room, a group of perhaps eight or nine of us in a circle of chairs, as we went through introductions with a little biographical detail about ourselves and why we were attending therapy. This was absolute torture to me. I know when I tried to say my name nothing coherent came out and I am sure when I ceased my efforts at talking nobody had understood a single word I said. Of the various levels of dysfluency on display, I know I was the worst.

The therapy centred on a process of slow smooth speech and easy onset. The theory was that the stammering blocks were caused by interruptions or stoppages in the airflow over the vocal chords. The proposed solution was to speak continuously on a breath until the breath was extinguished. So, for example, 'My name is Darren Benham' would effectively be enunciated as 'myyyynaaaameeeeeeeeeiiiii-sssssssssssssssDaaaaaaarrennnBeeeeenhaaaaam'. Each sound was elongated so there are no discernible pauses between the sounds or words thereby ensuring that the one continuous breath was all that was required.

The technique also incorporated easy onset so the problems many stammerers have with the plosive sounds such as 'b', 'd' and 'p' could be avoided by quietly skipping over those sounds and moving on to the vowel in the word. So, for example, my name would essentially sound like Arren Enham.

The end result was a flow of speech alright but it sounded very robotic and unnatural and required a vast amount of concentration. I had my doubts right away and therefore did not believe it would truly work. It ultimately didn't but that is the case for many forms of speech therapy that just focus on pure technique without tacking the other 90 per cent of the iceberg hidden under the water.

Although I had my doubts, I did experience an increased level of fluency in my speech – but not in really critical situations. Looking back, I do not believe it was the technique itself that generated the fluency but other factors, including the fact that I was finally doing something about my stammer, that contributed to my improvement.

We were given homework of reading aloud for a certain amount of time per day. We were also given reading material about voluntary stammering (where you stammer on purpose to effectively confront your fear of stammering) and your hierarchy of feared situations. I recall a one-on-one session in the therapist's office were she sat opposite me, monitoring me as I made a phone call using slow smooth speech. I was terrified. Terrified of revealing my stutter to the person on the phone and also terrified of how they would react to my prolonged silent blocks and pauses. I tried to utilise the learned techniques but my fear levels were too great. I simply could not produce air from my lungs over my vocal chords when there was so much adrenaline coursing through my body. I internalised that this technique could only work in limited circumstances where I was completely relaxed and in control, something that would never happen in the real world. I felt I was taught a technique that was inherently flawed.

I was not inspired to continue with this form of therapy. I did not like how I sounded nor did I want to continue with the practice. My feelings were common amongst the other participants but also, I found out later, indicative of the stammering mindset. Stammerers are experts in making excuses. We procrastinate and avoid undertaking speaking tasks, justifying the avoidance by stating we are too busy or not in the mood or, in my case, I did not like how I sounded. But I did not like when I blocked either so ultimately, looking back now, I did not have the courage to confront my speaking fears and I certainly did not have the motivation or application at the time to truly try the new techniques learned. It was only in 2005, when I did my first McGuire Programme course, that I believed a technique could work in the real world, but only if I had the application and belief to perfect the technique.

9

Growing Up

My brief stint at (ultimately) unsuccessful speech therapy reinforced my long-held belief that stammering was so ingrained into my consciousness and speech production mechanisms that there would be no improvement in my communication as I grew older. That realisation only grew deeper and the only method I knew to handle such dark thoughts was to throw myself back into the familiar world of sport.

In 2001 I received a phone call to go to a trial training match in O'Toole Park. The new Dublin manager, Kevin Fennelly, was looking at a few new players (I certainly was not new but I had been playing consistently well for the club for the previous few months) and keeping his options open. I thought about going back and whether I really wanted to be part of something that had indeed started out so good but eventually made me miserable. I wanted to return to the Dublin squad and give it another try because I felt I did not perform in my first few years on the panel and I knew I was better than that. Despite the club team enduring a torrid losing streak, I was hurling well and I had the mindset now that I had simply nothing to lose. What's the worst that could happen? Not be picked for the panel? Getting dropped? I had endured that before and knew what that felt like so I could play with real freedom and extract as much enjoyment as I could from this second opportunity.

The trial game went very well. Everything I attempted came off. For the first time among the county panel players I played like I had played for DCU and the club, and with absolutely no trepidation or fear of making a mistake. I had a different mentality. I left the pitch having enjoyed the game, satisfied with myself that I had performed to the best of my ability and honestly would not have been bothered if I had been told that I was not what they were looking for at that stage of the season.

The manager gathered us in the dressing room after the game and called out a list of new additions to the panel. My name was called. I was to attend training the following Tuesday and we would take it from there. Second bite of the cherry. There was no overwhelming sense of achievement, just a deep-rooted, ingrained sense of self-satisfaction that I had proved a few people on the panel wrong and that I was good enough to be around these players.

Outside of hurling, work was a continuous source of frustration for me. The company I was working for was under financial pressure and the environment was combative and stressful. I would go home at night and think about whether I had made any mistakes that day and mentally schedule the most urgent tasks to complete the following morning. It was exhausting. I decided to email a couple of recruitment consultants to determine if there were any possible opportunities for me and secretly began to plot my escape from Santry.

I massaged my CV, enhanced my practical experience and met with a number of recruitment agencies. I also met a specialist recruitment agent who worked with the Institute of Chartered Accountants and, despite my poor performance in a relaxed interview we had, he was confident of finding me a position in an accountancy firm, if I was committed to a career in accounting practice.

Hurling with the county team was finally enjoyable. I was performing well at training and got selected for a couple of National League games. I played the second last league game against Limerick in Parnell Park and though unspectacular I was solid enough to be selected for the last match, away to Offaly. I trained diligently by myself and spent a lot of time against the wall trying to speed up my swing and delivery, battling the encroaching nerves and self-doubt that started to inevitably envelop me. I was unable to sustain the positivity I had felt when joining the panel for the second time. I felt as if a clock was ticking, counting down to a dip in form or a poor performance that would justify the manager dropping me from the panel. I kept reminding myself to enjoy the whole process – the lead-up, the training, the games. I should have been thoroughly enjoying the whole experience but my negative self-talk and limiting beliefs would repeatedly resurface and undermine my confidence.

At that time, my club was playing intermediate hurling, which is a league below senior. I was the only guy playing intermediate level hurling on the Dublin county panel at that time. On the day we were to play Offaly, the club was due to play a very important relegation match against Trinity Gaels in the morning. I had to decide whether I was only going to play against Offaly in the afternoon and miss the club match or alternatively jeopardise my county performance by having some involvement in the club game beforehand.

I decided to play the club game on the basis that I was fit enough and that I would have some recovery time in the car journey down to Tullamore. I did not want the club team to lose that match and drop another league; it would have been disastrous for the club and the rest of the players. I played the club match and we won but it was a close match and I had underestimated how tired I would be afterwards. To make matters worse, the match had started late and there would be no time for a sit-down lunch after the match if I was to make it in time for the team warmup in Offaly. One of the managers of the club team had previously offered to drive me down to Tullamore and on the journey I consumed a banana and a bottle of Lucozade as my pre-match meal. I arrived at the dressing room ten minutes late, tired, hungry and poorly prepared for such an important match.

My legs started to loosen up during the warmup but during the national anthem I realised I was seriously dehydrated and I was also starving. I was going into this match ill-prepared and, at that level, if your preparation is not exact your performance with suffer and you will be punished.

From the start, we were under pressure. Long balls kept raining in on the full-back line and the Offaly forwards kept constantly moving. The Dooley and Hanniffy brothers were having a field day, constantly changing position and causing havoc. Our midfield and half-forward line could not stop their long deliveries. The goals started to come and we were losing heavily at half-time.

I knew I was struggling myself. I was second to the ball and my touch was not great. I had spilled an easy chance to pick and strike a ball which eventually ended up as a point for my marker. All the backs were struggling too but the full-back line was finding it tortuous. Early in the second half a long ball dropped in front of me. I had convinced myself earlier that if anything came down my wing I would just pull, connect with the ball and drive it further up the field. I wanted to get the ball away from me as far as possible. As the ball dropped, Simon Whelehan rushed in front of me, bent down and tried a two-handed jab lift to gather the ball. I was already in the process of completing my swing and noisily connected with the back of his leg. He cried out in pain, dropped his hurl and hit the floor. The referee rushed over and without hesitation withdrew a red card from his shorts pocket and presented it to me as irate Offaly players began to surround me. The perfect end to the perfect day. I walked off the field, head down, acutely aware of the jeers of the Offaly supporters, knowing my personal chances of playing for Dublin again were very slim.

I think we were beaten by around 20 points in the end. I remember the journey home in the bus being very subdued. No one had played well but I knew the full-back line hadn't performed as a unit and would be deemed to have been the primary reason for the heavy defeat.

I received a one-month ban as punishment for being sent off but continued to train with the panel. The next county match was the championship opener against Laois. As expected, my sending off was a factor in me not being selected for the first fifteen but I was named among the substitutes and was told to be ready to come on if any of the defenders suffered an injury or were playing poorly. The match was tight and low-scoring, with Laois eventually running out one-point winners in the end. It was another year of underachievement with the county team but the ending was a huge personal disappointment for me given all my hard work and determination to make a success of my progression to the county panel. I quickly got back to training and playing matches with the club, trying to forget my ignominious exit in Tullamore and the loss to Laois.

At the end of the summer, I received a telephone call from the Institute of Chartered Accountants' recruitment agent, who informed me that there was a position available in a small practice on the North Strand, if I was interested. No interview with the owner was required; I was told to report to the office the following Monday morning and get started. I thought it was unusual that no interview was required and only came to the conclusion after spending some time there that the owner was desperate to fill the position. I was initially very happy with the new job and worked directly with a patient and amiable audit manager who supervised my work and was instrumental in enhancing my practical accounts experience.

I was carefully spoon-fed assignments and various tasks of increasing difficulty and importance. I had no interaction with clients. The owner and audit manager attended most client meetings and any requests for client information I had were relayed to the audit manager and subsequently to the client. Inevitably, as I had very little verbal communication to perform, I shrunk further inside my comfort zones and would often pass the day without having said more than a dozen words. I quickly realised that time spent in such a restricted comfort zone as I had built is self-delusional. I was being handled delicately by my superior and I was making no effort to confront my stammering behaviours. I did not care. I envisaged that I would continue in my present role, indefinitely, grow old there, entirely satisfied with my limited periodic successes and monosyllabic existence. It was an entirely artificial atmosphere. Outside of work, whenever I had to speak – for example going to the barbers – I would stammer profusely, entirely unprepared physically and mentally for the actual act of speaking. I even felt that my vocal chords and every biological device required for speech production had grown weak, unused, out of practice and requiring serious, real-world workouts.

The problem was I knew this every time I had a severe speech block but did not have the courage or self-awareness to confront my stammer and perhaps choose a more noble and worthwhile existence of doing something about it. I convinced myself, absolutely and whole-heartedly, that I would find future ways out of having to speak, avoiding situations and sounds that caused me trouble. I wanted to stay enveloped in my comfort zone and didn't see any reason why I should attempt anything that risked the emotional fallout from stuttering. I concentrated on work, making ends meet and staying relatively sane living on my own.

Another year on the county team began and from the start there were huge time commitments involved. Friendly and trial matches were organised and played in Waterford, Kilkenny and Tipperary, and most of my weekends were spent on coaches, looking out the window, trying to avoid conversations and inwardly battling nerves and self-doubt. The confidence I had the previous year in being selected for important games and hurling well at training had evaporated during the off-season. I had even tried to keep a journal to note how well I had performed in county and club games in order to scientifically verify that I was able to compete at county level. I was always trying for perfection and had long since forgotten that I should have been playing for enjoyment and pleasure rather than obligation and necessity. Hurling with the club was also depressing. The team at that time were very weak and we would get regularly beaten by twenty-odd points. Players and teams that we used to dominate in previous matches were now suddenly made look like gifted athletes and hurlers because of our poor players and performances. If I personally didn't point all frees, execute to perfection every sideline cut and put in a huge number of hooks and blocks I felt a failure and that I had let the team down. When you are a county man and you play at intermediate level you are expected to dominate every game. I created that expectation in myself and it took the enjoyment out of every match and training session I had. I had been constantly playing hurling and football since I was eight years old and needed to revert back to the mentality of that eight-year-old boy, hoping for words of encouragement from Mr O'Keeffe in the school yard. I was currently playing like my self-esteem and self-worth were solely defined in terms of how well I played a match and how frequently the team won. Hurling and football were all I had; they were my creative and emotional releases but they were no longer bringing me the sustained joy to enable me to carry on through another day or two of living with the thoughts I was having and the reality of dealing with the consequences of doing nothing about my stutter.

I must have talked to the county manager but I cannot recall the specific conversation. Following an away match in Waterford, we were delayed coming home by coach and I made up to mind that I would not spend another weekend ruminating about something that was supposed to be enjoyable and supposed to make me happy. I left the county panel and rationalised that the reduced self-imposed pressure and extra time I would have to indulge in whatever I wanted to would force me to finally deal with my fragile mental health, my stammer and the issues that kept me up at night. In any event, I wasn't playing well enough at the time for the manager to make any serious attempts to keep me involved. I knew there were definitely no future chances to play county. I was in my mid-twenties and Dublin hurling was beginning huge underage structural developments that would pave the way for success at adult level over the next few years. There were better players playing at a higher level than me in Dublin and they deserved their chance of playing for the county.

It is very difficult for me to write about my relationship with my ex-wife simply because it is a deeply private matter and concerns not just me but also my ex-wife and our children. Before our separation, we shared a life together and we had children together. This book is not about the breakup of my marriage and there will be no salacious details of who said what and who did what to whom because that remains private. References to actual events in our relationship are not intended to create discomfort or embarrassment to my ex-wife but simply as events that occurred that divulge my stammering struggles, my descent into mental instability and current daily struggles. I intend to devote all my attention and references to key events that push my story forward and reveal details about my personality and my battles with my stammer and my mental health. Key facts, however, will be mentioned (and some purposefully omitted) and detailed without (I hope) judgement or subjective analysis on my part.

Like all couples in Ireland who had been seeing each other for some time, we succumbed to the temptation of getting on the property ladder. We met with banks, obtained a mortgage and bought a house in Swords in a new estate. All the while I was thinking that I should feel grown-up and burdened with obligations and financial commitments but in reality I was consumed with my own daily fears and inadequacies. My girlfriend recognised this and suggested I research something called the McGuire Programme. A relative of hers had participated in the programme some time ago with success and the programme had received some recent favourable media coverage on TV. I knew this was the final throw of the dice. I emailed my application to the regional director of the McGuire Programme and was accepted as a new student on the February 2005 course in Dublin. Finally, I was doing something about my speech.

My stammer in late 2004 and early 2005 was at its most severe. I had obtained a new job as an audit senior in an accountancy practice in north Dublin (having left my previous job on the North Strand, ostensibly to avoid the increasingly long commute in the mornings and evenings) but did not like my immediate superior and never felt comfortable there. My speech was barely manageable but was horrendous with clients on the phone and I spent my days thinking of ways to avoid any sort of verbal communication.

Looking back on the purely physical aspects of my speaking at that time, I would strenuously push through any speech blocks. I would use tricks (slapping my leg, using filler words such as 'ah', 'eh' and 'em') and always avoid eye contact. My headaches became increasingly severe and I developed ulcers principally due to the constant stress my body was in. Every time I needed to speak well, to be coherent, to be heard, my speech process failed me. I noticed that anybody to whom I talked became increasingly uncomfortable with my speech. They tried to finish my words and sentences and would always give me the 'take your time' line and nod empathetically. Countless people confided in me that it was ok, as they too had a stammer a few years ago and grew out of it or got over it or saw something on TV to help them and that sure, it will be ok. Pencils, pens and paper were constantly being offered to me as I became incomprehensible under any form of stress.

It's funny, but I liked it when people finished my words or sentences for me. It shortened my agony and their embarrassment, so for me that was a good thing. Other stammerers with greater dignity and self-respect may have the opposite feelings. I certainly did not enjoy the derisory smile I sometimes experienced or the obvious frustrations and impatience of some listeners. I became circumspect about other people's opinion as I grew older; 90 per cent of people I met were tolerant and obliging, 5 per cent were indifferent and the other 5 per cent I would have liked to assault.

Mentally I was at an all-time low. My stammer ate at my very being from the moment I woke to the moment I went to bed. I could not enjoy the happy personal moments in my life. I was getting married, I wanted kids, I had moved house and now that I was off the county team I was beginning to enjoy my sport (finally, again), but every thought I had was indirectly linked to my speech.

Most of all I dreaded the thought of having to make a speech at my wedding. In actuality, what I really dreaded was my new wife giving a speech at the wedding and 'showing me up' because deep down I knew I was too much of a coward to speak. I comforted myself with the thought that I was really thinking about my family and friends and how uncomfortable they would be, seeing me rigid with anxiety and struggling on every word. I was so deluded that I thought I was doing the honourable thing by opting out of speaking. I never thought about how my new wife would react or how understanding she must have been to agree to speak on my behalf.

As the time approached for us to formalise wedding plans and the events on the day we discussed the wedding vows. I simply had to choose the versions where all I said was, 'yes', 'no' and 'I do'. I had devised a plan with my new wife so that we would hold hands all through the ceremony. As I spoke, I would look across at her and she would mouth my words at the same time I would utter them and squeeze my hand, in time with me, enunciating the words. This was a trick that I had used in the past and, by God, I was going to use any trick I could to get through this ceremony.

On the morning of the wedding, I was nearly physically sick with the anxiety of saying my vows. My stammer had overtaken all my other emotions and until the ceremony was over I knew I would not be able to relax.

When it was time to conduct the speeches, a school friend of mine delivered a fine best man's speech. He made a joke about how I would not speak and that my gregarious new wife would undertake the speaking duties (as a sign of things to come, cue the laughter). Inside

I was absolutely dying. I felt immeasurably weak and a coward. I had put my own cowardice and fear ahead of everything and everyone on that day and any remaining ounce of self-respect I had was eroded in that moment.

All through my life I had developed the capacity to compartmentalise such emotionally disturbing events, position them into a storage facility in my brain and effectively think about them at a later date. I enjoyed my wedding day. I shouldn't have because I was a coward. The horrendous shame and guilt I felt because I did not speak was ostensibly forgotten but like all the instances with my father and all the times I failed to speak because of my stutter they are imprinted, forever, subconsciously on my psyche. Ultimately I know that I will have to experience a similar type of speaking occasion in the future and speak well to counterbalance that abject failure at my wedding. This is called 'cancelling' in the McGuire Programme and the term simply means that you replace negative speaking experiences with successful positive ones. In that way you begin to dissolve associated fear, guilt and self-hate and substitute with pride, self-fulfilment and satisfaction.

My wedding experience has at least provided me with the ability to advise stammerers on how to behave at their wedding receptions. I have advised people who are on the McGuire Programme (and who were seeking advice on whether or not to give a speech at their wedding) to say a few words at least. The blocks, stumbles and chokes are worth the sense of self-achievement and bravery and you will enjoy the rest of your day better knowing that you have stood up and faced down a huge fear that if you let it would make you feel like a failure for the rest of your life.

In the early stages of my involvement with the McGuire Programme, my wedding day silence motivated me to push through the barriers and obstacles that I faced to deal with problem words and sounds like my name and address. Subsequently, I often wondered what the people in the audience thought when they saw and heard my new wife speak rather than me. Did they equate that with a perceived lack of masculinity on my part? Did they even care or did they understand my reasons for not speaking? Did they honestly believe that I would have spoken at all given the severity of my stammer? I cared about what people thought about me that day but I did not care enough about what I would think about myself if I did not speak. Nobody advised me that I would feel this way; no one pushed me; no one inspired me to face my fears. Everyone just wanted me to have an enjoyable day and in order for me to do that the speaking obligations would be discharged by my new wife and not me. I thought about this for a huge amount of time.

From my wedding to the start of the McGuire Programme (February 2005), I undertook a period of deep introspection. I read as much as I could about stammering, especially the psychological aspects. I began to learn about the stammering iceberg, about how the physical struggles and blocks were only a fraction of the full impact the continuous stammering mentality and behaviour has on the individual. I began to read books on personal development, about expanding comfort zones, about becoming the person you want to be. I knew that there must be some redemptive path for me. I also knew I would be never cured from stammering but all I needed were tools to control it so that I could lead a life with my own voice and be free from the mental torture I was experiencing. I wrote down what my feared sounds and words were, what situations caused me the most trouble and I looked at *how* I stammered. I wanted to know what my body went through when I was blocking. I also noted what I was thinking during a block, what anxieties I had before and why I felt guilt, shame and self-hatred afterwards. I gathered as much evidence as I could about the monster inside me that ruled my life.

I discovered that the way my body reacted to anxiety and stress had a huge effect on my speaking performance. I learned about the power of concentration and how powerful the mind could be. I had read that many people could unlearn previous difficult experiences and replay them in their minds in a more positive framework. I had started to believe some element of control was possible but I did not even know where to start.

Then I joined the McGuire Programme.

10

The McGuire Programme

want to clarify some issues concerning the person I had become immediately before experiencing my first McGuire course. I certainly felt at that time that my entire life was a lie, a facade, and that the person who was visible to the world was not the real me. This will be difficult to understand, but my mind and soul, and whether I had conditioned them unintentionally (I have not figured that out yet), were on autopilot. Any social interaction I had, whether that encompassed work, playing sports or interacting with family and friends, involved me presenting an individual with a somewhat confident nature, secure in his own skin and focused on impending fatherhood. Inside I was black. Inside was dead. My first thought I had when I heard I was to become a father was I hope we choose a name that will be easy for me to say. I was pitifully self-centred. I had become such an introspective coward that I had to pretend to have the ability to function normally. I absolutely loathed my current job, finally coming to the conclusion that I had chosen the wrong profession – a decision I had based on my false expectation that I could earn money as a hermit-like accountant.

I knew deep inside me that something was wrong with my entire psyche and outlook. I could never enjoy myself. Everything I did became a competition with myself.

If I had a poor hurling match I would not eat or sleep for days after. I would over-analyse every mistake I made and try to rectify prior mistakes in the subsequent training session or match. Any negative comment at work would nearly bring me to tears. I was so consumed with my speech and my own shrinking comfort zones that I did not enjoy my early days of marriage and the time leading up to the birth of my son.

Socially amongst mutual friends I coped by becoming thoroughly expert at small talk, chipping in and interrupting to evade further questions, deflecting attention away from me and having no definitive feelings or opinions of my own. I was afraid to say 'no' because this would have involved me having to justify my opinion and invariably involve completing a sentence. At this stage a handful of words had become an insurmountable problem. Every positive emotion I had from previous speech therapies, self-help books, and personal research and analysis had evaporated. I later learned in therapy and from my own research that to sustain a strong emotional mindset and strong speaking performances requires huge work on your physiological and psychological self. It requires a certain voyage of self-discovery and self-awareness and constantly pushing out your comfort zones.

I was an empty shell of a human being, straining to go through the motions, displaying a false version of myself to the world. I fully expected to live my life like this, evading and anticipating any speaking occasions, working in a mundane field of my profession and feeling no one understood anything about the mental strain I was under. I was entering my thirties and absolutely did not know what type of human being I was. Inside I felt I *could* be outgoing and confident but felt a failure in my life. Sometimes I felt motivated to change things in my life but lacked the courage to undertake any form of action. I knew changes were necessary, but I was certain I was destined to continue with my current life and lifestyle indefinitely. I could see no hope for the future unless something radical entered into my life.

The first thought that struck me as I entered the large conference room of the Ashling Hotel in Dublin in February 2005 for my first McGuire Programme course was that the place was full of stammerers. There may have been about a hundred people there. Nobody had met me yet, nobody had talked to me, but it was the first time in my life I did not feel like an outcast.

The seating for the introductory speeches had been organised so that the new 'students' sat near the front, with returning 'graduates' and coaches nearer the back. I did not understand why the seating was positioned like this but I sensed the anticipation in the air. I could hear some of the graduates at the back, beginning their costal breathing. This is a breathing method used generally by singers (especially opera singers) that involves a voluntary raising and expansion of the diaphragm and a subsequent lowering and deflation to generate a more robust, reliable and predictable air flow. As taught on the programme, they were exaggerating the technique as a form of practice, but it was very disconcerting at the time. Some of them wore their belts (yes, belts originally designed to hold up trousers) tightened around their chests as a reminder to constantly breathe from the costal diaphragm. All these new observations would be explained in greater detail over the course of the next three days.

Up to that point in my life, I had never really been moved by a piece of literature, oratory or film. Some people would say that a poem they read really impacted their lives or that something that someone important said had changed the way they thought about a subject. When the course instructor, Martin Coombs, spoke, the hairs on the back of my neck stood up. This person was a recovering or nearly recovered former stammerer. He had had the exact same negative experiences and blocks as me, for the same number of years, and he was blowing the doors off the room with what he was saying. He had that something – that ability to grab your attention, to talk directly to you and to discuss issues that had made you cry yourself to sleep for many years in a way that made you feel you were not alone. That you were understood and that you were normal. He was not just fluent; he was a skilled communicator, invoking cadence and inflection to deliver key points and offer instruction. I was enthralled.

Martin proceeded to outline some of the topics that we were going to discuss, practice and drill over the course of the next few days but my head was spinning. However, I was very quickly brought down to reality. In order to gauge the severity of your stammer and as a means of assessing your performance over the four days, new students have to answer a series of interview-style questions, in front of an audience of about 100 people and have it video-recorded. I was not aware of this requirement on signing up for the programme, which was probably a good thing. I know I was one of the early participants, purely because I wanted it to be over. I was coming straight from work and was dressed in a shirt and tie, which somehow looked odd amongst this group. My group of first-timers were an eclectic bunch, mostly younger than me, mostly male, all evidently terrified of being video-recorded.

The questions included what my full name was, mobile number, age and favourite football team. I know I lied about three times with my sisters' names, my mobile number and my favourite football team. When I had left the hot seat, I congratulated myself on a superb display of controlled evasion and avoidance. When I watched my video back a few days later I realised the display of blocks, filler words and long pauses were evidence of someone who not only had a very severe overt stammer but who was completely deluding himself over a very long period of time.

Although I was to become a coach and a course instructor intern on the McGuire Programme I am certainly not a staunch defender of all things McGuire. The programme was and continues to be a great source of help for me. It was the first place that supported me in any meaningful way with my stammer and provided me with the knowledge and tools to undertake the journey in controlling my speech. The descriptions and details of the changes that occurred in my speech processes and more importantly in my mentality towards my stammer and myself are entirely my own. I would encourage anyone who wants to learn more about the programme to do so. Success or failure in dealing with stammering is dependent on so many individualistic variables that I would hesitate to rate any therapy or programme over another. I think I was lucky in that the programme suited my needs at a time when I needed it, providing also the motivation and support to do things I would not ordinarily do.

Costal breathing is the foundation of the McGuire Programme. The basic principle is that the normal speaking process, which originates for most people in the crural diaphragm, has been contaminated in stammerers through years of bad speaking experiences and deeply ingrained learned bad habits. The quickest way of bypassing this malfunctioning process is to speak from the costal diaphragm, which, when employed, results in a more powerful and reliable production of air flow. The McGuire Programme teaches that the crural diaphragm is connected to a nerve running down the spine which is triggered by fear, stress and speaking performance anxiety. The theory is that by eliminating all dealings with the crural diaphragm the existence of these psychological issues is largely redundant.

Speaking from the costal diaphragm involves speaking at the top of a costal breath. A costal breath is generated when a full inhalation of air is obtained from raising and expanding your rib cage voluntarily. When the rib cage has been raised and expanded to its maximum, that is the perfect time to speak and air is generated as the lungs and rib cage deflate.

A crural breath occurs normally and naturally for everyone, they just breathe. But to generate a costal inhalation requires concentration, practice, timing and knowledge.

To be honest I do not think I had any difficulty with learning the basic technique, including the breathing. I was lucky in that the graduates teaching me were of a high standard, plus I was being instructed by, in my opinion, the greatest instructor on the programme. Once I had become convinced that not only control but a certain eloquence could be achieved by using the techniques I became very motivated. Slowly, during the course of the first day, I started to perfect the breathing technique, incorporating sounds and words into the process, and I could say my name to the person opposite me without any difficulty for the first time in my life. This was a very gradual process over the entire day, starting from saying one-syllable sounds to your first name, then surname and finally your entire name.

At the end of the first full day of the course, the instructor gave three new students an opportunity to stand up, in front of the entire gathering of graduates and new students, and state their name.

For many stammerers, their names are the most difficult words to say. There is such an emotional charge surrounding your name, of expressing who you are, that many stammerers always block or struggle with it. For me, I always had problems with the plosive sounds (p, d, b) so my name, in my own mind, was particularly difficult to say without stammering. Buoyed by the early successes I had that day in conquering my name, I took the opportunity of stating my name to the entire group on the Thursday evening. When I stood up, there were so many conflicting emotions going through my body. I was filled with historical negative self-talk and fear. My body was running through the usual response mechanisms of trying to prevent my impending block by convincing me to sit right back down. Every bad speaking occasion in my life where I totally messed up saying my name was running through my brain. My heart rate rose and a huge part of me wanted the ground to open up around me. I was going to try a new speaking technique that went completely against the learned process that I used for my whole life. I felt it was a huge task to complete; I felt it was like willing your heart to beat in a different way.

But little changes had taken place inside me and in my conscious-ness. I knew nobody was going to judge me. I knew I would not have a negative audience reaction. I had said my name before to other graduates without problems (although never to a group of people). I had begun to trust the technique and I was highly motivated. My desire to speak well greatly outweighed any compulsion I had to sit down and shut up. I stood up, back straight, eye-balled the instructor, took a full costal breath, concentrated on my exact timing and with authority stated my full name. Martin was pleased, applauded me, and I sat down. He looked upset. Did I do it wrong? No ... I was to stand up again and he got the entire room to applaud me while I stood there for a good minute and accepted a room full of praise, handshakes and encouragement. I had achieved something momen-tous in my life. That was the first time I had said my entire name in 29 years without a speech block.

Throughout the course of the next two days we were introduced to the various McGuire Programme techniques and tools. We were first taught the checklist, which is a list of all the overriding indi-vidual components making up speech production using the costal breathing techniques. Another session (usually interactive with the strong graduates) detailed the rules, laws and directions which reminded us of the continuous need to push out our speaking comfort zones, to cancel poor technique and other various tenets that we would need to employ if we were to become adept at using the new speaking technique and to continue to become eloquent speakers when we left the bubble of the McGuire Programme.

It is difficult to remember all the new concepts at the first course, so these are reinforced through attendance at subsequent full courses, attendance at regional support meetings and constant communication with your assigned personal speaking coach. I later learned that the single most important technique that new students were designed to learn on their first programmes was the basic cycle of speech, which is pause, breathe, speak and release. Pausing before speaking gives the speaker time to formulate what they are going to say and prepares them to employ the individual components of the McGuire technique, which is essentially speaking at the top of a full costal breath. The breathe section is simply taking a full and fast costal breath. We then speak with authority and power from the diaphragm, and then we release any residual air through the mouth when we have finished speaking. There are many other components that finesse the process, and it is much harder to employ success-fully in practice than theory, but there is no doubt it works.

All through these days I was constantly speaking to different coaches and graduates with the technique, breathing from the costal diaphragm and coming to terms with my potential and endless possibilities.

The Saturday of a full McGuire course is dedicated to preparing the new students for street contacts and public speaking. A street contact involves initiating a brief conversation with a complete stranger. Precipitated by an assertive 'Excuse me' to draw the stranger's attention, a street contact could be something like asking for the time, asking for directions or indeed a disclosure. A disclo-sure involves giving the stranger your name, the reason why you are stopping them, the fact that you were on a speech recovery/therapy course and thanking them for their kind attention and time.

I was thinking about the street contacts process during the very first second of my McGuire course introduction on the prior

Wednesday evening and, like all stammerers, I was scanning ahead and fearing the worst. All my past experiences and the knowledge of my redundant speaking process convinced me that I could never achieve the lofty goal of 100 street contacts. If this was not bad enough, following the street contacts was public speaking, where the new graduates were encouraged to stand up on a soap box in the middle of Grafton Street, state their names and state the purpose for their weekend stay in Dublin.

The only reason I was able to begin to attempt the street contacts and public speaking was because there had been a huge change in my psyche and speaking intentions during the duration of the course and because of the preparatory work done on the Saturday morning of the course. As a result of the successful speaking experiences I had achieved during the weekend, I was able to rationalise that I could repeat these experiences once I employed the same tools and techniques I had learned. I had grasped the new breathing process, I understood the very basic elements of the McGuire technique and I now only required the requisite amount of courage and self-confidence.

That self-confidence was enhanced by specifically designed speaking exercises run by a number of experienced McGuire coaches on the Saturday morning, called the Harrison workshops. The workshops were designed to demonstrate effective communication skills and how much fun could be had from speaking. All through my life, speaking had been linked with terrible consequences and associated memories. Throughout this morning I was to experience pleasure in speaking. I would also learn techniques such as adding music to my voice, appreciating the power of a good pause, voice projection, and using my body as added tools in my new speaking process armoury. My self-confidence and assuredness grew with every speaking occasion and all the coaches and other graduates provided further encouragement with their kind words and compliments. When it was time to go and hit the streets of Dublin I felt I was ready (gulp, gulp) to give this new speaking process the proper application it deserved.

New students are always paired with an experienced McGuire coach when they go out for street contacts for the first time. My coach took me aside, gave me further words of encouragement and took me through what I should say for the first few contacts. This was an attempt to clarify as many things in my mind as possible before initiating a street contact. The fewer items to worry about the less that could go wrong.

I remember I had trouble with the first few contacts, especially with the 'Excuse me' part. I was choking out the words, not being assertive enough and not speaking at the top of a breath. My coach was always emphasising the importance of the next contact, which prevented me from ruminating on any perceived failed contacts and focused my attention on implementing the physical technique. I continued with it and was happy with my progress. Each contact became increasingly less terrifying, thanks to the kind people of Dublin. No one commented on why someone with such a strong Dublin accent wanted to know the directions to O'Connell Street.

I achieved 67 contacts and three disclosures in nearly two hours walking between O'Connell Street and Grafton Street, politely inter-rupting strangers, asking them for the time and directions to the particular street we were going to. These contacts were certainly not perfect and would not be good enough to pass the coaching test (on future McGuire courses) but the bravery it took to do them came from inside me and provided me with great confidence that I could replicate that courage in the future. If you want to be technical about it in terms of speech production, I used a few filler words, like 'eh' and 'mmm', and pushed past a few blocks (continuing to produce air during the struggle to vocalise a sound, which you were taught not to do on the programme), but these were inevitable given my initial low base level and the short time frame from learning the technique in a secure environment to employing it in the real world.

The public speeches are somewhat of a blur. The speeches were to take place outside Dunnes Stores at the top of Grafton Street. A gaudy banner and soapbox were positioned and the course instructor proceeded to rally as many people as he could from the passing shoppers to stop and gather round as they were about to witness something extraordinary. With good articulation, voice projection and enunciation he proceeded to tell them a little about the programme and why we were going around the streets of Dublin, and then he invited the new graduates (including me) to do the same. I think I was one of very first up, perhaps even the first one. I was filled with adrenalin and purpose and was roundly applauded by the McGuire community who surrounded the soapbox. I said my name (perfect) and told everyone where I was from and why I was here (I was on a speech recovery course to help me control my stammer). I thanked everyone on the programme who had helped me so far and then stood down to wild applause and cheers, not just from the McGuire people but also appreciative shoppers and natives who had stayed to watch mine and everyone else's speech. There were no blocks, chokes or silent blocks or repetitions. I was very assertive, using voice projection, and my desire to speak greatly outweighed any desire to hide my stammer. I had a thoroughly positive speech outlook when I stood up to speak and that was reflected in the quality of the mechanics of my speech.

I looked on as each new student took their turn and did something they could not have imagined they would do in their lifetimes. Lifetimes are defined by such treasured moments and that was one moment that will stay with me forever.

Walking back to the Ashling Hotel from Grafton Street was a very emotional experience for me. I had done something that I had never thought I could do, given the self-imposed limitations and constraints I had forced upon myself all my life. I had faced my greatest fears and conquered them, and was at last armed with the raw materials and guidance to continue to fight my stammer and relegate it to a secondary issue in my life as opposed to the overwhelmingly debilitating one it always had been. However, I was under no illusion that I was cured, and I had realised very early that the method demanded constant practice and dedication. Stammering was not simply a bad habit I had developed over the years; it was an endemic self-destructive addiction that had ravaged me. I had been addicted to self-doubt, avoiding words and situations, and punishing myself. Physically I was also addicted to pushing out words and sounds, using filler words, avoiding eye contact and constantly trying to hide my stammer, which was blatantly obvious anyway whenever I spoke. I rationalised after my first McGuire course that I would have to face breaking these addictions and realistically it was going to take everything I had to do so.

11

The Reading

The first few months after your first McGuire Programme you feel dizzy with expectation and excitement for the future ahead. All sorts of thoughts and ideas previously denounced as impossible due to your stammer suddenly appear tangible and within touching distance. That dream job, which you've always wanted but didn't even apply for because of your speech – can't wait for the interview. That pretty blonde in work you've been waiting to ask out – no problem, let me talk to her. Reading bedtime stories to the children – dig out *The Gruffalo* and let's go. You feel as if there is no upper limit on what you can experience and achieve now that you have (1) said your name without blocking for the first time in your life, (2) spoken to 100 strangers in an hour on the street and (3) given a public speech in a crowded city centre location and followed that up with a gut-wrenching, emotion-filled farewell speech to your closest friends and family on the last day of your first McGuire Programme.

After my first course, I certainly felt that stammering would no longer dictate my life and that if I followed the rules and directions, coupled with diligent practice and application where I could employ the tools and techniques, then the programme's goals of self-actualisation and eloquent speech were eminently obtainable.

The atmosphere in the Ashling Hotel for my first course weekend was overwhelming positive and nurturing (it has to be to change a lifetime of negative thinking around speaking). I had met and was being coached by exceptional individuals who, to me at least, sounded entirely free of stammering both within the confines of the programme but, more importantly, able to live their own (now) self-determined lives without the mental and physical manifestations of chronic stuttering.

I read the accompanying manual that comes as reading material in its entirety during the first two days of my first course and came to the conclusion that continued success and progress could be made with my speech if I employed the same discipline, diligence and work ethic that I wholeheartedly displayed over the four days of my course. However, I quickly became aware that my admittedly now extraordinarily positive mindset towards my stammer over the course of those first few days was beginning to revert to type. I was not putting in the dedicated hours of practice as I did on the course and I was not in the epicentre of a community of people actively demonstrating and using the costal breathing technique. I spoke to my coach and he reassured me that this was normal as I slowly came down from the emotional and liberating high that speaking properly for the first time in my life generated. My reality was going back to work and dealing with the impending birth of my son. It was inevitable that my technique and mental focus would deteriorate – I was not applying it for fourteen hours a day constantly over three days. I would have to learn how to sustain that positive mindset and strong technique in the real world, which is anywhere outside the safe confines of a course, support meeting or refresher day.

The sports mentality analogy immediately resonated with me when I was introduced to the basic tenets of the McGuire Programme. The theory is that speaking, and speaking eloquently, is like learning an entirely new sport for stammerers. And, like any sport, to become good at it requires knowledge of the technique and the motivation and desire to train at that technique, over time, so that it becomes habitual and almost automatically employed. This was entirely logical to me and I immediately recognised the similarities to a skilled sport like hurling. Hurling, even when the fundamentals are acquired, demands constant practice and drilling, enhancing muscle memory and skills acquisition so that on important occasions (matches) those learned skills can be applied.

Over the next few weeks I memorised the various checklists, laws, rules and directions and undertook a daily regime of two hours of speech-related practice. This included, for me, highly charged emotional phone calls to my own coach and other coaches on the programme. The phone was always a desperately hideous instrument for me, but the support and encouragement shown to me on my first course gave me the determination to confront my fears. I followed the advice of various coaches who told me to make numerous short and concise phone calls to other coaches and to various hotels, pubs and restaurants, working on my feared words and sounds.

I realised quickly that the first stage in my recovery was mastering saying my name on the phone calls to the coaches. This was the first major obstacle and after many failed attempts my coach and I mastered a technique where an assertive emphasis on the D of my first name would carry me over, with the same breath, to say my full name. Every day there were successes obtained, challenges set and met, and the technique was becoming habitualised. I enjoyed going to the support meetings tremendously. At that time most of the attendees were either coaches or course instructors and I listened intently to their advice and comments on how my speech was progressing.

I attended my second course in Waterford three months after the Dublin course and this is where I learned the nuances of the technique and reinforced the basics of costal breathing. I was disciplined and knowledgeable and took many occasions to speak in split sessions held for refreshers and more experienced graduates of the programme. My second course inspired me to set myself a goal that would motivate me to continue my practice and hard work and at the same time start to create positive affirmative speaking memories in my mind, replacing the years of negative ones already ensconced there.

With the help of my coach, I decided to set myself the goal of doing a reading at my son's christening, which was a couple of months away. The memory of not speaking at my wedding was still etched into my psyche and I knew that if I had a good speaking performance during the christening that it would go a long way towards repairing my self-esteem and lay the foundations for strong continued speaking performances in the future.

Around this time too, I began reading a book by John Harrison called *How to Conquer Your Fears of Speaking before People*. It was recommended reading by the coaches on the McGuire Programme. The author was a chronic stutterer and over time evolved to become a fluent speaker, losing all mental and physical manifestations of stammering. The book chronicles his story and how he drafted together a framework for understanding how certain stimuli in his own life and immediate environment impinged upon his mind and ultimately his speech. However, the parts that I was mostly interested in, in advance of my reading, were the chapters devoted to conquering the substantial fears held by stammerers of speaking to groups of people. The book details various techniques and tools to employ to connect with the audience and become a strong and powerful public speaker. There was so much to learn but I knew from hurling that I had to focus and master the basics of any new skill first before progressing to finessing the techniques and elevating myself to their advanced stages. So I focused on improving the fluidity of the movement of my costal diaphragm, ensuring my chest fully expanded as I took a full breath and spoke with power and authority as I hit the first sound of my four words per breath narrative. When my four words were completed I then concentrated on releasing all the remaining air in my lungs, depressing my rib cage and related muscles and pausing for a few seconds to think about the next repetition of the cycle and how I wanted to say the next four words.

This cycle is called the basic cycle of speech and is fundamental to the McGuire Programme. For the purposes of the reading I ignored all other tools and techniques and felt that if I could master the basic cycle then I could deliver the Mass reading in a controlled and powerful fashion, which was my only expectation at the time. During the support meetings in the intervening period I was constantly pushing myself, willing myself to talk at every opportunity and constantly feeling the discomfort of doing something that had been alien to me for so long. The simple act of maintaining eye contact while speaking was an insurmountable challenge to me as during my previous extended speech blocks my eye contact would go completely and I would invariably glance at the ceiling or floor, anywhere but the eyes of my listener. I did not want to see the look on my listener's face when I blocked repeatedly or choked on sounds. I spoke with my coach about my intended reductive approach to the techniques I had learned on the programme and he was also satisfied. I kept things simple too because the less I had to worry about the less could go wrong.

Over the remaining weeks till the reading I practiced every morning and every evening. I would sit down in front of a full-length mirror and initially practice my breathing. I opened my mouth, expanded my rib cage and inhaled deeply, elevating my chest cavity and rib cage as the air filled my lungs. When my rib cage reached its maximum extended position I exhaled slowly, reversing the process and pausing for ten seconds before repeating the cycle. During my practice sessions I always wore a belt around my chest, tightened enough to stay in place but loose enough not to constrict my breathing. When I felt the belt tighten as my chest expanded I knew I was employing the technique correctly. When I felt I was in full control over my breathing, I introduced words at the top of the breath, starting with one word, then two and finally up to four. I read aloud from the programme manual. I read aloud from the newspaper and accounting manuals. I read my Mass reading, quickly memorising it to ensure there would be absolutely no confusion when the time came to stand on the altar and deliver my performance. I rehearsed the speech in front of my wife and subsequently with my coach at the support meetings. I rehearsed in the car going to work and over the phone with coaches. The continual repetition of the physical act of reading improved not only my technique but also my mindset. As I spoke I felt the tone and timbre of my voice change. The register also got lower and I was speaking deep from my chest. The pausing brought authority and purpose to my words. Every night in bed I visualised *how* I was going to speak and imagined myself in front of the unsuspecting congregation, breathing, speaking and pausing, and constantly reinforcing the belief that I could achieve my speaking goal. John Harrison's book recommended adding intonation and music to my voice when I spoke and emphasised the power that pausing makes in public speaking. I was scared and constantly having to battle my default mental position of negativity and fear of failure and public humiliation, but the more I practiced the easier it appeared to push these negative thoughts away and replace them with positive ones.

On the morning of the Mass, my wife was busy preparing our son for his big day while I made the finishing touches to my speech. All through the previous weeks my focus had been entirely on my speech but unfortunately that was the effort required to overcome a lifelong stammer. If my reading turned out to be a disaster then my recovery would effectively have been stalled until I cancelled that experience with another future successful one. The stakes were huge for me personally. I needed this occasion to go well to justify all the hard work and provide conclusive evidence to the captive audience that I was recovering from stammering.

There were a number of families in the church that morning christening their children. I mistakenly believed that mine and my wife's family would be the only ones present but I had prepared so much physically and mentally for the reading that in truth it did not disrupt me. I was wearing my favourite navy suit, with the belt of my dressing gown across my chest under my shirt. All the other belts I owned were bulky and patently visible under my suit, and so I reverted to the much thinner and almost invisible dressing-gown belt. I felt the satisfying tightening of the belt around my chest as I tried to warm up before the reading, expanding and deflating my lungs, going over the narrative of the reading in my head. All through the early stages of the Mass there were various times when panic reared its familiar face but I quickly replaced these thoughts with the mental images of victory and success that I had practiced in front of the full-length mirror for so many weeks.

When the readings started, I watched and listened as various other parents and family members delivered their lines. I was nervous but nowhere at the level of previous speaking situations where panic had a vice-like grip around my chest and vocal chords and the realisation that I was going to fail enveloped me. Over the previous few weeks I had learned to deal with fear and panic through concentration and courage, and I felt confident the technique would work in any pressurised speaking situation.

When it was my turn to read, I approached the lectern slowly and waved the standing microphone away. I would not need it. For weeks in support meetings I had practiced delivering lines with good voice projection and articulation and knew my naked voice would reach every dark recess of the church. I looked up at the audience and gave a slight smile. Something felt wrong, unnaturally alien. There was no sweat, no pounding heartbeat, no blurred vision. There was only a simple clarity and the excitement of an impending successful speaking situation. I had practiced for so long the four words per breath cycle that I reduced all confusion in my own head about the way I was going to speak. Fear plus confusion equals panic. There was *some* fear but I was not confused and there certainly wasn't panic. I was ready to begin.

Something happened to me up on the altar that I can never explain. When I began my breathing cycle and expanded my lungs, all fear of speaking dissolved. I felt that I was on my own, in my room, looking at my reflection in the mirror. I just spoke. No technique, no costal breathing, just spoke the way every normal speaker does. I became almost casual, introducing a cadence into my speech that I never thought possible. I inflected certain sounds and paused for gravity and purpose not because I had completed my basic cycle of speech but because John Harrison said that strong public speakers did it. I checked my cufflinks as I spoke. I felt as if I could talk like this forever. I looked at the words on the page not because I needed to remind myself of them but because I did not want the audience to see the incredulity on my face. It was an entirely out-of-body experience. In mid-sentence I looked over at my family and smiled, specifically to my mother, as a display of supreme confidence and happiness. Deep down I knew I had the ability and tools at my disposal if I came across a troublesome word or sound but I never needed them. I had that safety net, which obviously boosted my confidence, but I had drilled and practiced for so long that my mind was just used to hearing me speak in a controlled and powerful fashion. On this one occasion my mind just got out of its own way. I recognised the musicality of my own speech and how I emphasised certain words for effect. I didn't want the reading to end.

When finished, still on the altar, I took the piece of paper with the reading on it and placed it in my suit breast pocket and joined the small group of other readers to the side of the altar. I just stood there and looked out at the audience, trying to determine if they could tell if I had a stammer or whether they recognised the effort and practice it had taken for me to deliver that performance today. I knew the majority of them probably were not even listening, caught up in their own arrangements and plans for their respective special days. I was hugely satisfied with what I had done and had not let the coaches and my fellow stammerers in the support group down. They had convinced me that I could achieve my goal and I kept thinking to myself what was the next thing I could do to push myself even further?

As I walked towards my extended family, my mother looked up, winked at me and mouthed silently that she was proud of me. My sisters congratulated me. My sister-in-law leaned over and said that 'no one would have ever noticed' – which indicated to me that there was no discernible trace of any stammering in the reading. I did not know how to take that statement. In one way, I was prepared to speak mechanically and very obviously using a technique to control my stammer. However my body just wanted to express itself after years of struggle. Even the priest caught me as we were leaving the church and said I had read very well.

My success that day brought me a very tangible taste of what living a normal life would be without stammering. I wanted more. The reading convinced me that I was on the right path and that if I focused on my speech entirely then similar speaking successes could be obtainable in the future.

Unfortunately, it was never going to be that straightforward.

12

Turbulence

I continued my daily practice rituals and attended every support meeting held for the first nine months after my first course. I also called my coach daily and tried to kill my fear of the phone through continued practice phone calls to hotels, gyms, restaurants, pubs and other establishments, working on certain feared words and sounds and generally using the basic techniques to habitualise them as my new speaking processes. I was also doing twice-daily breathing exercises and reading aloud (using full technique) for hours on end.

I was delighted with the progress I was making in McGuire situations and with the McGuire coaches, though it was a lot more difficult to claim any successes in the real world. Despite the success of my reading at the christening, I had a huge mental impediment in believing work to be an environment in which I could speak as powerfully as I did on the altar. With public speaking, the power is entirely with the person on the podium or the individual with the microphone. If those variables are shifted somewhat then that would trigger an entirely different set of self-perceptions and beliefs that would consequently affect my relative fear levels and attitude toward speaking and ability to employ the techniques I had learned. The difficulty I was experiencing and slowly coming to terms with during my initial tentative steps in recovering from stammering is that every single speaking situation is different – public speaking is different to a job interview, is different to a phone call, is different to a McGuire Programme support meeting. I had not yet grasped or understood that a consistent universal McGuire Programme approach was needed in *all* situations. In my naivety and inexperience I focused all my efforts in initially gaining success in the McGuire world (meetings, refresher days, courses) as opposed to having to face the painful process of incorporating my technique into the work environment, where inevitably there would be (at least in my own mind) conflict, judgement, assessment and direct consequences for not speaking well.

I still had major problems with acknowledging myself as a stammerer and, at first, did not want to use my technique in work or social situations because I sounded very slow, mechanical and, in my own head, abnormal. Despite the overwhelming evidence to the contrary, I always historically believed that when I spoke no one could discern I stammered. It was only when I watched videos of myself speaking (like my McGuire Programme first day video) that I recognised what exactly others saw when I was in the middle of a speaking process. As well as practising and refining a new physical speaking technique I would have to entirely accept to myself that I was a stammerer and that stammering (either in an out-of-control involuntary manner or in a McGuire Programme controlled and demonstrable manner) would remain part of my speaking processes for a long time.

This problem of applying the technique in the real world would continue for many years to come.

My son was born in March 2005. I was using every available moment of spare time to practice my speech and looking back I did not prioritise my responsibilities as a new father. I tried to support my family as much as I could but my personal commitment to defeating my stammering monster took up precious hours.

I was undergoing huge transitions in my life which created conflict. I was addicted to the successes I was having in the McGuire Programme and consumed by the problems I was having in employing the techniques in work and to lesser extent in my daily life. Work and routine became a hated distraction for me. I did not have the emotional intelligence at the time to calmly self-analyse my progress to date in the context of being a husband or father and appreciate the other responsibilities I had incumbent on me. Daily inconveniences triggered vast emotional outbursts, of frustration at my perceived speaking failures, of resentment at other stammerers who were obviously taking their techniques to the real world, and self-directed anger at the deterioration of my relationship with my wife. I was sick of the constant knot in my stomach, the dull probing pain in the back of my right eye that signalled the arrival of another migraine and the continuous chalky taste in my mouth from painkillers.

My headaches were becoming more severe and would sometimes continue right through the night until the following day. I was also experiencing severe pressure in work – deadlines, unrealistic demands and an utterly all-consuming hatred of my job, my career and everything to do with accounting. At that time, I mistakenly believed that my involvement with the McGuire Programme was the only positive thing in my life. Even sport had taken a back seat. I had effectively given up hurling for a year to concentrate solely on my speech. Every evening after work I rushed to the spare room to practice my speech, wear my belt, begin my breathing and transport myself to a place where I was beginning to be recognised as a success, a model student, a fine exponent of the technique. Speech practice was prioritised over hurling training time and I could not envisage simply turning up for matches at the weekend and hoping to play well.

I knew that if I adopted this approach (just playing matches at the weekend without having to put in the necessary effort of training all week) I would destroy myself mentally with self-criticism and my entire weekend would be spent starving myself as punishment for not playing well. I wanted to spend my time practising my speech rather than hurling training because I genuinely believed that if I gave it two years of my life then I would be free forever to accomplish and experience anything I wanted in a stammering-free life.

My life at that point was consumed with trying to defeat my stammer. All waking moments in my life for the past 30 years had been spent reflecting on or thinking about my stammer, its implications and how I was going to carry on for the rest of my life with this debilitating handicap. I had found something to at least control it and I embraced it with open arms. I was presented with this opportunity but I did not how to properly make use of it. I could not harness it, manipulate it to work holistically for me, to help me improve my lifestyle and relationships and to achieve self-actualisation. Others seemingly could and that frustrated me.

In October 2005 I went on a staff training weekend in Galway to become a primary coach on the McGuire Programme. This involved a weekend of speech evaluation and a written exam on the various McGuire Programme teachings and principles. The weekend was very enjoyable. I was immersed in my comfort zone with people I enjoyed spending time with, and working towards something that I first dreamed about on the Wednesday evening of my first course. I passed all tests and was eventually put on the phone list of coaches. I could not wait to receive my first call from the new crop of students who were beginning their journeys on the McGuire Programme.

For the first two years after my first McGuire course I continued with my practice schedule, attended support meetings and made full use of the support network. I built up a strong circle of friends at the support meetings and we constantly encouraged and challenged ourselves. We would facilitate the meetings, we attended staff training weekends together and we would even organise to meet up in town at the weekends for contacts. Some of us engaged in ad hoc public speaking sessions in Trinity College, really trying to push out our comfort zones and becoming strong speakers. We would stand in the middle of Trinity College and urge people to gather round and listen to us as we said our names and briefly shared our stammering journeys. This to me was not real life. There were no consequences if I didn't speak well – perhaps a few disgruntled tourists who would walk around the corner to queue for hours to see the Book of Kells. It was somewhat self-indulgent but it was practice and I felt that ultimately it would transition to speaking gains in the real world (such as ringing the dentist to arrange an appointment and, of course, speaking well at work).

In the McGuire environment I was bulletproof. On subsequent courses I would make disclosures to a bus full of passengers in Cork, and in Galway I walked into a McDonalds and proudly informed everyone (with good technique and voice projection) that I was a recovering stammerer. Some coaches believed I was showing off and I got some flak on the programme, but these were incidents that were spur of the moment and reinforced my belief that I was well on the way to beating the monster inside me.

These performances clearly indicated the dichotomy in my reasoning at that time. I had the confidence and belief to go onto a bus full of passengers and disclose to them that I was a recovering stammerer, and yet I could not get through a phone call in work without stammering uncontrollably. Outside of the programme though, it was so much more difficult. I had trouble employing the same confidence and assertiveness. The work environment was so much more stressful, fast-paced and demanding that it was my perception that no one would wait for me if I took a pause. My adrenalin levels would immediately spike when I started work in the mornings. It was frustrating not to have the command over my speech to the same extent as in the McGuire environment, but I rationalised that the gains I was making in the McGuire world would eventually translate to the working environment. The other hurdle in work was that I was not performing well; I disliked the managers there and certainly did not feel comfortable enough about raising the issue of my speech with anyone. Looking back, I did not have the requisite levels of energy or bravery to transition the use of my technique in McGuire situations to work. The situation in work may have been different if I was a well-respected senior member of staff or performing stellar work in bringing jobs in under budget and on time. I simply found the work environment very difficult at that time, not just speech-wise but also in fulfilling my own work expectations and targets that I had set myself.

My health was seriously failing me, my headaches were becoming debilitating and I was convinced I had chosen the wrong profession. I did not have the courage to speak with full technique in a busy open-plan office and I never discussed the programme with my colleagues, which is essential for implementing the McGuire Programme into your daily life. In work, I reverted to my old stammering self. A switch seemed to go off in my brain whenever I crossed the threshold of my job that made me lose all motivation to use the valuable techniques I had learned to control my speech.

This was a deeply troubling problem for me and brought on another level of frustration and anxiety. I was inherently unhappy in work, with the people there and with the jobs I was doing. Arriving home after another stressful day I would be on edge, impatient and truculent, and feeling that no one understood my predicament or mental state.

Outside of work though, finally I was noticing some marginal speaking gains – for instance in ordering food, going to the cinema and in general being able to express myself more coherently. I did a very successful radio interview on *Newstalk*; I had an article published about me in the *Northside People*. These were successes because they were within my comfort zones. I was talking about stammering, it was evident I was a stammerer and therefore there were no repercussions for the self-disclosure. The audience *expected* me to use a technique when I talked simply because I was living proof of the benefits of using same. What would have really been a success was if I had told my manger in work that I had attended the McGuire Programme to deal with my stammer. At that time, I simply could not do that.

The situation in work troubled me greatly. I had this mental block about being open with my speech and about using any form of technique there. My perceptions and beliefs about my speech were entirely negative and this was why I was so reticent about taking action in work. I spoke about this on the programme, at courses and in support meetings and it appeared to be a common problem with the majority of people on the programme.

The really successful graduates, who actually took their tools and technique to the real world, all told me that it would take time and patience and a lot of bravery to be as successful in work as in the confines of the programme. They suggested I talk to my boss, explaining the techniques to him and why I would need to regress to speaking mechanically in order to avoid the speech blockages that my colleagues had by now become used to. I knew this was something I would have to eventually overcome if I was finally to become free of stammering where it mattered most.

I was becoming resentful about the amount of work I was having to do on my speech to now not only maintain my speaking gains but also to just be able to say my name without a block. Stress is very often the leading cause of speech relapse. However, I could not rationalise this at the time and instead ramped up my practice times and worked even harder to continue to push out my comfort zones and overcome my remaining obstacles, unintentionally creating more stress for myself. The little speech successes I had outside of the work environment tantalised me with the possibilities of what I could achieve.

However, I was starting to fade. I had responsibilities outside of the programme with my family and work and I was frustrated that I just could not spend time working on my speech. I needed to take a step back and re-evaluate my progress and take some time out before planning my next speaking adventures. But I didn't. I was so afraid of reverting back to my old stammering self that I ploughed on.

Around the beginning of 2008 the severity of my headaches and stomach problems elevated to such a degree that I started to become addicted to over-the-counter painkillers. I would take them at the very first sign of an impending headache and ended up in a cycle of reliance and dependency that affected my day-to-day functioning. I lost a tremendous amount of weight and had to go to the toilet maybe fifteen times a day. When the migraines came they would reduce me to a heap, lying under the covers in the bed, protecting myself from any light. I spoke to my doctor, who put me on blood pressure medicine to reduce the frequency of the migraines and steroids to slowly come off the painkillers. I was by then taking up to ten pain-killers a day. At that time, I could not swallow the pills so I would bite and chew them and eventually swallow them with coke; every other option made me vomit. I remember many nights staring at the clock, wishing the pain would go away and that I could grab some sleep before the next working day. The medication prescribed by the doctor did little to reduce the frequency or severity of the head-aches. I was immersed in this cycle of stress, headaches, medication and lack of sleep. I was stressed from work, relationship issues, my weight loss and general failing health, and often during the periods when it felt that my head was being split open with an ice pick I would conclude that either I would die from the current pain or kill myself because I could not face a future with the continued severity and frequency of my headaches.

By late 2008, my involvement with the McGuire Programme started to diminish. Everyone who completes their first course usually achieves speaking gains and sufficient momentum in the first two to three years to battle most of their speaking demons. However, it is very difficult to remain on top of your speech in all situations when you have other commitments and you don't have the support network at work to continually force you to use your techniques.

Like most graduates, diminishing returns had set in. I was by now a course instructor intern on the programme and the next step on the McGuire ladder was instructing a course. I was a coach and advising new students on how to perform the techniques and encouraging them to push out their comfort zones when I was struggling myself in the real world. My speech priorities changed. I was disappointed with myself for not completely overcoming my stammer where it mattered most – in work. I began to beat myself up about the apparent lack of speaking success there.

I had recently changed jobs (I had simply walked out of my last position) and unsuspectedly landed into a very highly pressured environment with very dominant personalities and perpetual dead-lines. I knew myself, early on, that I didn't have, at that time, what it takes to successfully integrate my McGuire successes into the work environment.

I determined that a break from the programme would be best in the long term for my speech. I figured that the absence of the safety net of the support meetings and courses would push me to find answers to my inability to incorporate the techniques in the real world and that the time previously devoted to McGuire practice should be expended on my family.

13

Reunion

The latter months of 2011 were some of the most difficult and traumatic times for my physical and mental health. I was losing weight rapidly and my daily work and training regimes were being decimated with severe and continuous headaches that enveloped the entirety of my skull. My marriage was under strain at this stage and I felt deep within myself that something was seriously wrong with me, healthwise. I *looked* different. I didn't recognise myself when I looked in the mirror in the mornings. My face was gaunt and my physique had atrophied. I was not handling the daily work pressures incumbent on someone in my position in work. I was not sleeping because of the sustained headaches that sometimes endured for up to four days at a time. I was chewing over-the-counter painkillers like confectionary and my stomach was constantly upset and nauseous as a result. I desperately needed someone to talk to and obtain some clarity as to why my health was so bad at that time. I knew myself that my stammer needed to be addressed and worked on but I lacked the motivation and desire to do anything about it.

I thought a lot during this time about ending my life, not in a grandiose display of self-importance but as the next logical move to remove the pain and suffering in my life. I had simply endured too much. I woke up every morning with the realisation that I was going to endure a severe headache or migraine for a series of days. I was working in an environment where I struggled every day to remain focused and dedicated while my mind was rebelling against any increase in stress levels by constantly demanding my body to get up, walk out the door and never go back. I was still dealing psychologically with stammering, particularly the emotional consequences of avoiding speaking situations, principally in work. The familiar cycle of guilt, self-hate and shame would resurface as I continually let my stammer dictate my behaviours and rule my life.

I was not particularly enjoying hurling either. I was being played out of position and it seemed as if the club manager was just trying to accommodate me, out of a misplaced sense of loyalty or from the fact that I had simply been around the place for so long that it was inconceivable he would drop me. I remember matches where I would barely touch the ball and everyone would laugh and hint that I was on the way out because I was in my mid-thirties but I knew, deep down, that the tank was not empty yet and that I could still hurl at a level I was satisfied with if I could just get my head sorted and deal with the issues that were destroying me mentally.

Sometimes I would wear my old college jersey or college shorts to training or under my club gear at club matches just to *feel* like I was playing for the college again. I was trying to recapture those fleeting number of matches in DCU when I actively loved playing, when for that hour nothing else mattered in the world and I felt I did my best for the guys around me. Playing for the club was highly pressurised during this time. In reality the pressure was always self-imposed and if I did not play well or play to a level I had predicted that would inevitably lead to some self-imposed physical punishment like running in the afternoon after a match, starving myself or replaying in my mind every strike, touch of the ball, catch or pass I made in the match to critically evaluate my performance and determine how I could improve. I used to assess my performances and award myself marks out of ten in a little black notebook, in which I would also set goals to achieve at the next training session. Hurling was no longer about enjoyment or a release from daily life and a means of self-expression. It was now all about justifying my place on the team, attaining a higher self-critiqued grade than the last match and to simply not fuck up in a match.

My mental health at that time catastrophised everything too. I was not simply unwell; I was actually going to die. My migraines were, in fact, fatal brain tumours. My weight loss and muscle atrophy were certainly cancerous. Everyone at the club shared the opinion that I was finished. People at work knew I could not handle the pressure. Everyone I spoke to knew instantly about my stammer and defined me as an incoherent, incompetent idiot. I was thinking a lot about my childhood too and that how for such a long period of time there has been struggle in my life that had not dissipated the older I became. In fact, I knew I was actually becoming more self-destructive as time wore on because of my inability to deal with the negative thoughts being self-generated and my ignorance of my mental condition.

I wanted to recreate those four years I spent in DCU because I knew that I needed something or some event to sustain me. My resolve to deal with my mental illness was eroding and deep down I knew that drastic action was required. I craved some form of relief from the daily physical and mental pain I was in and I logically concluded that if I could create a similar environment to my college years then perhaps I would develop the mental strength and acumen to discover the reasons for my ill-health and ultimately, much like stammering, learn the tools and techniques to just even control the affliction when it rears its head. I suddenly wanted to reconnect with everyone on the teams I had played with, to see how they were, to catch up and maybe, just maybe, see if we could reproduce the magic and enjoyment that was produced when we all played together. The idea motivated me just to be around long enough to see it come to fruition. I was excited and started to connect with as many of the lads as I could through social media and email. Over the weeks the communication web extended. Everyone seemed fine, dealing respectively with middle age and families and the daily grind of living their lives. They all were happy to reconnect. When there was a sufficient number to field a team, I sent a general email to the group and enquired about the possibility of meeting up and perhaps, tentatively, fielding a team against the current DCU hurling team.

The responses slowly came back, filled with complaints about aching limbs, recent retirements, hurleys lost in the vast recesses of cluttered sheds and apprehension about going into combat against individuals fifteen years younger. I appeased them with reassurances that the current team would take it very lightly and respectfully against us and that really it is only a quick runaround and no one has to go into cardiac arrest. Yes, I acknowledged we are all in our mid-thirties and yes the current DCU are very good and yes helmets are compulsory now.

Organising the reunion meant having to make contact with the current DCU hurling cub and relevant committee and I did this through the magic of email and its ongoing gift to the stammerer of not requiring any verbal interaction. I proudly explained to the relevant individual that I was a member of that famous DCU side that made it to the Fitzgibbon Cup weekend in Cork in 1997 and that the guys and I would like to have a reunion in DCU with the possibility of perhaps, tentatively, a friendly match with the contemporary hurling team. The email remained unanswered for a couple of days and I questioned whether it was a good idea of mine on a selfish whim to involve so many people in something that could potentially fall flat on its face. Eventually, the email was responded to with an enthusiastic affirmative reply and confirmation that the current hurling set-up would be delighted to host us and face us on the battlefield once certain details like team sizes and times, etc. were ironed out.

I then became a facilitator for a few days, proposing dates and times for matches and inevitably some dates did not suit some while suiting others. The match was eventually arranged for a Saturday afternoon in October. I reckoned that the conditions would suit us better as the heavy pitch would slow the current team down a little and, anyway, the mid-90s group were used to college hurling in the middle of winter (albeit 15 years ago) and October would be positively balmy for us.

Things began to get serious. I did not want to disgrace myself in front of my contemporaries or the opposition so I conducted a few sessions against the hurling wall in the club and enhanced this with a number of timed laps around the club pitch. At least the hurl would be in my hand for a few consecutive days before the match, which was always important to me.

For days leading up to the event the group emails started to fly, old pictures suddenly resurrected with slimmer, leaner and less wrinkled versions of ourselves appearing. Tales of injuries, foul strokes, victorious matches, wild nights out and drunken bus trips resurfaced. This was more like it.

The Saturday of the game we had arranged to meet up in the (new to us) Sports Complex at the base of DCU campus. The guys started to drift in, gear in hand, wondering whether this was going to be a success or not. Familiar faces drew smiles and handshakes and incredulity that so and so was still hurling or had retired or had even gotten married given their wandering eyes in college. The topic of the match and the opposition was repeatedly raised but I tried to reassure everyone that no one would get hurt and that, once again, the current DCU guys would not take the piss. We had a huge advantage too in that Seán Óg Ó hAilpín had agreed to come and would meet us closer to the throw-in time outside the dressing rooms across the Ballymun Road. Óige had by this time become a legendary figure not only in hurling circles but also in modern Irish culture generally and was a hugely recognisable figure. I was concerned about him wandering around outside a vacant dressing room on the Ballymun Road but he was a big boy and could take care of himself.

We made our way to the dressing room and I started to relax and think about the match. Some players who had confirmed their attendance did not show but there were thirteen or so hardy individuals, reeling back the years, while a couple of others, dogged by current or historic injuries, watched expectedly on the sideline.

I drove up to the dressing room and suddenly caught a glimpse of Seán Óg drilling a sliotar against the dressing-room wall. I knew it was him by his distinctive wristy back swing of the hurl as he stroked the ball and caught it immediately on the rebound from the wall. There were loud greetings and requests for one of his three senior All-Ireland medals and he quickly became one of us again, another potential victim of slagging and practical jokes.

In something reminiscent of the way the mid-90s team operated, the current outfit had forgotten to bring the DCU away jerseys for us. However, a set of jerseys from the local Whitehall GAA club was produced and we reluctantly togged out in the white and red colours of one of my club's (Scoil Uí Chonaill) rivals. I got a bit of stick for the jerseys too, everyone knowing how passionate I was about my club and the difficulty I had in wearing any colours that were not my own.

The dressing rooms in the new facilities were not what we were used to. Back in the 1990s we always changed in the rustic conditions of the last dressing room in the main Sports Complex, never knowing who was next door, the ladies' rugby team or the men's hockey team. I had hoped I'd feel like it was 1995 again in the dressing room and I wasn't disappointed. The physiques had definitely changed (apart from Óige) and I wasn't as self-conscious about my toned-down physique next to some other guys who had liberally enjoyed the finer things in life post-DCU. I was asked about the guys who could not make it and stories were told concerning these absentees and their related match performances/post-match antics/female associations. We promised to have another reunion in the near future and try to ensure that a suitable date could be found for everyone on the group email.

We took to the field in our alien jerseys and (despite my advanced warnings to wear navy blue shorts) our obviously ill-fitting and multi-coloured shorts. By general consensus it was agreed that someone with three All-Ireland medals should know what he was doing and therefore Óige was bestowed with the responsibility of conducting the warmup. When I say warmup, I actually mean drilling the ball from one side to the other while remaining stationery and a couple of short runs to the middle of the pitch and back. I looked over at the opposition and they appeared to be taking it more seriously, with the addition of stretching to their warmup repertoire. One of their guys was going to ref the match but he remained motionless, standing in the middle of the pitch and staring at Seán Óg as if Jesus Christ had come down from the cross and was carrying a hurl. I roared at him to get the game going as some of the guys were seizing up already. Some of them had ominously started to breathe very heavily and lean awkwardly on hurls that had not seen the light of day for ten years.

There was no team selection as such; everyone played roughly where they played in college. I played around midfield, Seán Óg in the backs, Duggo in goals, Farrelly, Lanigan, Duff and MacCriostail up front. Henderson, Teu (Óige's brother) and Tom Neville floated around the place, picking up loose balls. DCU were respectful but competitive, their players still trying to comprehend that they were on the same field as the Cork superstar. Duggo was busy and back to his usual best in goal while Tom Henderson upheld his Kilkenny lineage with some typical stylish play. Tom Neville was busy and industrious till his infamous fitness issues resurfaced and he had to regrettably retire and lie down on the sideline. Our forwards all relived their youth, all lively and deadly in front of goal. Ciarán MacCriostail was especially prolific, despite playing with what looked like a misshapen axe from the 1920s. He certainly was carrying off that retro look. Seán Óg was majestic, oozing class and intelligently minding himself for his next big match with Cork. I enjoyed every second. I remembered the way everyone hurled and hit the ball and nothing had changed. Everyone moved and sounded the same way as they did in the mid-90s. The intensity may have dropped but I knew instinctively what the other players would do simply because I had played with them for so long.

The game was conducted in good spirits until a current DCU player tried to upstage me by trying to flick a ball over my head as he was running past me. I learned long along that there is a certain etiquette in dealing with established players and one thing you should never do is flick a ball over someone's head and not expect to get a slap. The player ran past me, flicked the ball and tried to gather it again as he overtook me. I instinctively raised my hurl to his helmet as he met my shoulder and there was a loud clatter as the ash of the hurl met his plastic helmet. He let out a roar and screamed at me and I stood my ground, smiling at him, reinforcing my belief that he was trying to make a fool out of me. Some words were said but none in malice and we eventually shook hands and played the rest of the game trying not to go into heart failure.

The mid-90s guys took the spoils that day but realistically we wondered whether the current DCU team had been really trying. They magnanimously asserted that they had indeed tried their best and we were happy with that and stood around for a while after getting to know the current players and having pictures collectively taken for future slagging on social media. I was happy that the spirit and sense of camaraderie held by us in the mid-90s had been sustained by the current generation. They all seemed genuinely thrilled to be playing us and evidently loved playing for DCU as much as we did in our prime.

After a well-earned shower and debriefing session we all headed back to one of the new bars in the college for some drinks and food. Further long-lost stories were revived and everyone agreed the event was a success and definitely something that could be built on in the future. At least everyone now had contact details for everyone else and I encouraged all the lads to remain in contact with one another.

During the afternoon I had got talking to Bryan Duggan at the bar (Bryan and I don't drink) and he asked me where I had gotten the idea for the reunion from. I told him that I was ill and that I felt I was going to die and so I wanted to see everyone again for one last time. I don't know if he thought I was serious or not but those were my selfish motives and for one afternoon I was not thinking about my stutter, my health or my deteriorating mental state.

Teu Ó hAilpín also approached me and said something that seemed very profound at the time. He told me that when I talked now that I 'had no more stutters'. I thought about this for a long time after the event and realised it was an external acknowledgement of the progress I had made in my speech due to my involvement with the McGuire Programme and from my own self-sacrifice and hard work. It also reaffirmed to me that I was absolutely delusional in my own assessment of the state of my speech in college because I honestly felt I was managing with my small talk and avoidances to conceal my stammer from everyone back then.

As the evening wore on, those with responsibilities, families and long journeys to make began to drift away. I thanked everyone for coming and making the effort despite all their current commitments. I was satisfied that everyone was happy and had enjoyed themselves and that the event ran smoothly. I was grateful to the current DCU guys for playing the game in a generous spirit and embracing the occasion. It was great to be around these guys again and appreciate each other's company, at least for a short while. There were some guys I would have loved to catch up with who couldn't make the trip but I was sure that with a little bit of persistence and peer pressure from the other guys future reunions would have greater attendances. For now, that was enough for me.

14

Someone New

The reality I was faced with in late 2011 was not a pleasant one. Ultimately my marriage deteriorated to such an extent that I had to leave the family home with no immediate contingency plan in place while having to simultaneously deal with my deteriorating physical and mental health. Having to leave my children destroyed me.

So in November 2011, I return to my parents' house in tears, not for myself but because I always told my children I would never leave them and would always protect them and look after them. Sure, all parents say that right? But when I said it I always meant it. I mean, even when I was married I did not want to go out at night or have a night away because I had made that promise to love my children, internally, externally, telepathically – that I was there for them always. So, after midnight on the fateful night I return to Portland Row, I am sitting on my mother's couch crying because if the children woke up in the middle of the night I would not be there and because I had broken my promise to them. Years later, that separation, that absence and those multiple years' worth of broken promises is knifing my heart, burdening my conscience and burning my soul.

I returned to Portland Row simply because my finances demanded it, but there was also the feeling that I needed to be around people who would look out for me and somehow deep inside me I had a distinct atavistic desire not to be alone. I continued to fall apart on my mother's sofa, and I clearly discerned at that time that I did not handle my imminent return to my mother's box room at all well. My thoughts revolved around the children and when I was going to see them next and I thought about the explanation my ex-wife would have to give to the children explaining my absence from the house. I remained on my own for much of that night, ruminating and considering various options and approaches to dealing with my current troubling situation. Everything I had ever worked for and anticipated as being part of my life was now gone. I remained emotionally numb for a long time, finding it difficult to formulate any sort of conventional plan of action to deal with the events that were beginning to unfold in front of me, but I knew one thing and that was that the next few months were going to challenge me with obstacles I had never experienced before in my life.

After falling back into my mother's arms, certain behavioural patterns re-occur, patterns that can only appear when a son returns home. Hurling gear gets washed, beds are made and hot meals are provided. I need all the looking after I can get. I'm in a bad way at this stage. The absolute gut-wrenching agony of not hearing my kids first thing in the morning or hearing them sleeping in the next room is beyond comprehension. I have continual nightmares of 'bad' things happening to my kids, of 'bad' people doing 'bad' things to them. I see these acts, these actions, but somehow I am tied down, restrained; they are calling my name, I can hear them but can't respond. Jesus Christ, I can feel my mind slowly unravelling, all logic, all rational thoughts are seeping out through my ears. There is a physical hole in my heart.

I see the children frequently but very briefly. Before school; after school. My ex-wife and I discuss a schedule. It is important, she says, that the children get used to a schedule for the benefit of everyone (but what about me?) so that they can cope with the separation.

I delineate my days into clearly defined timeframes and prepare myself mentally to get through each designated phase as best as I can, trying not to think about the children. I haven't internalised yet that I have no future, haven't thought about where I'm going to live, finances, etc. Phase one of a day is to get to work and operate functionally ... dress myself and look reasonably alive ... and focus on numbers, maths, working papers, nice neat lines, red pens; this page looks nice; I need Tipp-Ex. It seems a long way to the end of Phase 1 (10.30 a.m.). Made it; Phase 2 begins, always with a trip to Tesco beside work ... treat myself to an apple, can of diet coke and a croissant ... return to work, eat at my desk and check the clock. 10.35 a.m. ... haven't thought about the kids in five minutes ... that's good. What the fuck is wrong with you, not thinking about your kids? Look at the screen, ok, the bank reconciliation does not balance ... sort this out.

At this stage of the day I find myself getting ratty, tense and uncompromising but I manifestly restrain myself from punching people square in the face as (a) I need the money, (b) I don't want to go to jail and (c) that would upset the kids (at some level).

Then the time came when I did not want to return 'home'. At this stage, my mother and father had separated (nothing formal, he just left some months previously) and he had moved to live on his own in Mayo.

I was sleeping in my sister's room (she was away in college) but on her return I would sleep in the spare bed in the box room. I simply did not want to spend any time sleeping or residing there and so on many nights I would stay out late driving or alternatively return to my office around midnight to complete assignments, read professional updates or simply search the internet for stories of similar people in similar circumstances.

The first month of the separation allowed me the time to think about what really happened. For the first time in my life my speech was not the all-encompassing issue on my mind. I realised that the life I had mapped out for myself after I got married had completely gone and at 36 years of age I had to confront issues like possible homelessness, making ends meet, establishing and maintaining a routine with my children, finding a way to communicate with my ex-wife, staying sane, holding down a job and formulating a plan of action to get me out of my mother's box room.

My migraines had become a bit more irregular with the use of new medication from the doctor but they had not disappeared. When they did come they could cause severe stomach problems, unmerciful pains across my eyes and temples, and incapacitate me for hours. There were occasions where I would pass out from the pain and wake up on the floor of the toilet, my underwear around my ankles, thinking to myself Jesus Christ, so this is how I am going to die, just like Elvis. At these moments I would also think of my children and how they would react to the news. That memory would spur me to get off the floor, throw up the remaining contents of my stomach and spend the rest of the night or day in bed with the covers over my head, shaking uncontrollably and sweating profusely.

I logically wrote down the various problems I was having and decided to try to tackle them individually. I was crying myself to sleep at night, missing my children, not having them run into my bedroom every morning like they used to, and frantically trying to simply function at work so as not to make a huge mistake that would jeopardise my position. It was essential that I maintained my finances and continued to contribute to my ex-wife and children. I also surmised that I would need finances to eventually leave my mother's house and start my life again.

Looking back, the only reason I got up in the morning was to be able to see my children. I had overwhelming urges to quit my job and bury myself under the covers of the bed and never come out but the thoughts of my children kept me going. At that time there was no defined access schedule and I tried to see my children as often as I could. However, on the days I did not see them I really struggled to maintain my sanity and I would spend the whole night thinking about them, wondering if they were missing me and whether I should simply return to the family home and demand to see them.

A month after I left the family home, I confessed to my manager in work that my marriage had ended, that I was living with my mother and that, honestly, I was having a hard time processing what had happened. My performance in work had definitely dipped; I was truculent and I had very little patience with anyone at that time. The managers were very appreciative of my honesty and they recip-rocated with kindness and understanding.

All through my career I struggled to enjoy work and thinking back there was no job where I felt completely happy and settled. In the early stages of my career, I definitely lacked practical expe-rience and struggled early on. I quickly learned a few harsh realities after making some mistakes with other people's money and always felt pressure at work. I eventually progressed to being a manger in another job which brought its own pressures of dealing with staff and being directly in the firing line of the partners. All through my marriage I had complained about wanting to leave my job but I could never figure out what I actually wanted to do. My stammer limited my options tremendously, which brought its own frustrations, and I was disgusted with myself that I did not have the courage or drive, even after the McGuire Programme, to try to do something that would make me happy. In reality though, I did not know what I really wanted to do. I struggled with trying to define who I really was at that point in time. I was a qualified and experienced accountant who did not like his job (despite being surrounded by a supportive and understanding team) and did not like accountancy. I was a married father but only had scheduled access to his children. I was in my mid-thirties but living in my mother's box room. I had successfully battled my stammer with the help of the McGuire Programme but had walked away from it because it did not bring the results I wanted fast enough. I did not know who I was, where I was going and whether I actually wanted to carry on at all.

I drafted a list at midnight one night, under the faltering overhead light in my car, of what I needed to do and should do in order to progress with my life. The list was literally constructed on the back of an envelope but during the seconds it took me to write out the list I was not thinking of my children or missing them. The list was necessarily concise and in no order of priority, importance or practicality:

1. Be happy
2. Stop the migraines
3. Stop thinking 'bad' thoughts about the children
4. Get more money
5. Make your children proud
6. Don't be lonely
7. Get out of the box room
8. Return to the McGuire Programme?
9. Don't listen to sad songs
10. Get through the days
11. Get through the nights

12. Don't pass out in the toilet
13. Find someone else

The last thing on my to-do list was actually the first thing I achieved. I knew that I needed someone in my life who would support and love me for me and whom I could love too. I hate being on my own but on many occasions I crave my own company. Sometimes I want someone to be there just for me but only on my terms and on call for when I selfishly need them.

I met Astrid after a couple of attempts at online dating. I knew very quickly that I wanted to be with this person and for her to be a major part of my life. We discussed our mutual past histories and surmised that there would be many problems ahead but we felt stronger dealing with life together.

I went to the doctor following a severe migraine attack where I had collapsed and passed out on the floor from the pain. At this stage I was heavily depressed and lacked any motivation to work or to get out of bed in the morning, and getting through the day was becomingly increasing more difficult. I was not suicidal. I was empty. It was if my whole life force had been sucked out of me. When I looked in the mirror I absolutely hated what I saw. I was disgusted that I had ended up in this position. I confessed to Astrid how I was feeling and she advised me to speak candidly to the doctor about my mental health and the problems I was having simply functioning.

The doctor diagnosed me with suffering from cluster headaches, which are the most severe form of migraines, and introduced another set of medication into my daily regime. I was also diagnosed with severe separation anxiety from the children and depression, and was prescribed rest and antidepressants.

During this period I was just about able to last a working day if I broke it down into clearly defined units of time, and I congratulated myself after every fifteen minutes for not strangling someone, walking out or making a huge mistake. Astrid and I knew that we required the finances to live together and to at least start to try to save — we both knew that ultimately I would have to spend thousands on legal fees. Divorces are not cheap.

The toughest part about being separated was not being able to see the kids first thing in the morning. I had horrible nightmares where I would hear the children scream out my name and I would be chained down, unable to move while their screams became increasingly desperate. I would hear them say my name everywhere, even at work, and it would take a huge physical effort not to break down and cry. Whenever I thought about them my heart would wrench. When I saw them at the scheduled access times I tried to be as positive as I could but I was always dreading the time when I had to return them to their mother. I would attempt to remain impassive as I waved to them as the door closed shut while inwardly a ragged knife was gutting my insides.

I spent as much time as I could with Astrid. We talked about the kids and how best to deal with my increasing separation anxiety. We also talked about my physical and mental health. Astrid was particularly interested in alternative therapies like mindfulness while I only had a rudimentary knowledge of these things. At first I was dismissive and reluctant to embrace them but my headaches were so bad and frequent I would have tried anything.

I did not like the potential side effects of my prescribed antidepressants, which included possible reduced cognitive ability and mood swings. I continued to play hurling and exercise regularly and that provided a good distraction from the marital issues. However, I was obviously depressed about the children and how my life had turned out. I was enveloped with this all-pervasive malaise about everything. The times with Astrid boosted me and sustained me for the forthcoming working day where I would desperately try to do my job and pretend everything was fine.

My speech at this time was functional at best but I did not care. When I stood in front of someone, blocking badly, the only thoughts going through my mind concerned my children. Perversely, there was a slight improvement in my speech as I did not give a fuck what people thought about how I stammered. My most pressing problem was trying to keep mentally stable enough not to just walk out of my job and to be there for my children when they needed me.

When the first legal letter arrived, I just broke. I was reading the letter in the kitchen having come from a particularly gruelling day in work and I felt like a barrier had burst inside me. The thought genuinely occurred to me that this is the final straw; this is the thing that is going to push you over the edge and destroy you. Try getting up in the morning now after this.

The letter itself was not the catalyst: it was the accumulation of my childhood traumas; my struggle with stammering and the related self-hate, embarrassment and guilt; my marriage ending; my separation from the children; and now this.

I remember feeling diminished and I could not think of what to do next. Astrid and I discussed the letter and how we were going to approach this. We gathered our thoughts and decided that despite my sparse finances I had to confront these issues and engage my own solicitor.

The ramping up of legal proceedings coincided with another deterioration in my mental health. I had changed jobs a couple of times over a nine-month period, at the end of which I decided, for my own sanity, that I would try to become self-employed. The aim was to generate commensurate income working by myself, on my own terms, in my own created environment. Astrid and I listed out all the issues we needed to tackle in order to enhance our quality of life together. I was now heavily reliant on Astrid. When I had a headache during scheduled access times she would mind the kids. She would try to keep me relaxed when I thought too much about the cost of legal proceedings, and she would always encourage me to look to the future and imagine our life together when these issues were finally resolved and in the past.

There were many difficult times. Astrid called an ambulance to the house one night when I collapsed in the toilet. I had hit my head against the wall while unconscious and when I woke I was lying on the floor with Astrid holding my head in her hands. She became frightened when I was unresponsive for some moments and had called the emergency services. The stress and psychological distress were triggering an increase in the frequency and severity of my headaches.

My nights were filled with nightmares about my children and my father. I would frequently wake up in the middle of the night screaming profanities while Astrid would quietly try to placate me and get me to fall back asleep. I had frequent panic attacks and would not know where I was. I would ring Astrid to say I was lost or that I had parked my car and lost it. I definitely had diminished cognitive ability and it took massive amounts of energy for me to keep concentration and to focus on even the smallest tasks.

Astrid and I decided to focus on my health, and particularly on the migraines. We cleaned up my diet, increased my water intake, tried to increase my time sleeping and saw a different doctor who ultimately referred me to a neurologist. The neurologist was very good, but very expensive. He wanted me to have an MRI but at this stage I was paying legal fees and I could not afford it. He took an extensive history and insisted I tried to wean myself off over-the-counter painkillers and Frovex (which I had been using as my primary painkiller for some time), which was highly addictive. He surmised that I was chemically addicted to these drugs and that many of the headaches were created by my body in order to satisfy the cravings my brain was simulating. He also recommended various stress reduction techniques like yoga and mindfulness, and told me to continue with my efforts to clean up my diet. However, the most common migraine triggers he told me to avoid I stayed away from anyway, like coffee or orange juice. He ultimately suggested that it was in all probability stress-related and I had to deal with the under-lying issues causing the stress in order to live with fewer migraines.

Increasingly, my moods became very unstable and I would experience vastly contrasting emotions over a very short period of time. I would argue with Astrid and become very aggressive and then the next minute the red mist would clear and I would apologise to her. I understood immediately I was behaving like my father but was absolutely powerless to stop it. I would crave attention from Astrid but when she spent some time with me I would be resentful over something I perceived she had said or didn't do and I would argue with her. My emotions were always so much deeper. I would feel hurt more. I would feel joy more. When I thought about my kids, I would laugh and then cry moments later. When I thought about my father I would feel sorry for him and the next moment want to murder him.

However, there was one incident that made me re-evaluate my behaviour and mental state. There had been a disagreement in work that day and I came home conflicted and furious with myself for not having the social skills to resolve the problem. The kids were over at the time and I took offence at something my son had said, so I cut him off mid-sentence. Astrid reproached me and told me to calm down and that my tone was unacceptable.

I felt immediately betrayed and stormed out of the room. Astrid intervened as I began to raise my voice and get extremely agitated and distressed. Astrid told me to go upstairs and I completely broke down. If you looked objectively at the situation I completely blew it out of all proportion and took things from a comment that was never meant to cause offense. But I was completely manipulated by my feelings at that time. My behaviour during the legal battles was entirely governed by my emotions and similarly this event had caused my emotions to go into hyperdrive. I tried to rationalise what had happened but I couldn't. I suddenly wanted to feel pain, to feel something different to what I was feeling then. I looked around the room and saw a pen on the cabinet beside the bed. It seems totally ridiculous now but I picked it up, stuck it into my left wrist until it penetrated the skin and scratched a few inches along the length of my wrist until it bled. If there was a knife in the room in all probability I would have killed myself.

When my wrist started bleeding, it was as if I was looking at another individual undertaking this weird act. I was seeing someone – a complete stranger – cut his wrist because his partner said something he did not like. Logic, reason, common sense all became redundant.

I spent an hour crying, looking at my wrist, and thinking to myself that I was turning into my father. My emotions had completely overtaken me; there was no rational part of my brain functioning. I was disgusted with myself but I also realised I needed to speak to Astrid about this so that we could undertake a plan together to resolve these issues.

While I was struggling to keep my emotions in check, Astrid was constantly on the internet, trying to figure out why I had cut myself and why I was behaving the way I was. I rationalised that I was under stress from the court case and I was worn down by the daily headaches and feeling constantly ill. I just needed a break.

Astrid read about various conditions like bipolar, manic depression and borderline personality disorder, and one night we decided that I needed to start seeing a psychologist, counsellor or some professional just to talk to and try to alleviate my mental distress.

My emotions had governed my behaviours all my life and the past problems I had with my relationships, my social interaction with people, my fear of abandonment and my mood swings could stem from genetics and childhood trauma.

Astrid made an appointment to see a psychologist while we continued to deal with the escalating court case. The final hearing was in June 2016 and included a morning in court where I would have to represent myself. At this stage I had spent thousands on legal fees and I could no longer afford legal representation. All morning I blocked and stammered my way through the judge's and opposing counsel's questions while trying to make my points that I was a good father and that I was contributing as much financially as I could. The only good thing about that day was that the divorce was finalised and for now at least there would not be any more legal letters.

15

Final Game

Sport, and in particular hurling, has been a hugely influential and affirming part of my life. Unfortunately, in my late thirties there was a sudden deterioration in my fitness levels and ability to play through pain that brought the stark reality of impending retirement sharply into focus.

I knew after the first hurling match I played in 2015 with my club that it was my final year playing. I was running after my direct opponent and the muscle in my left hamstring tore. It was not a serious tear and certainly not my first hamstring injury, but I was so disappointed with the frailties of my body that even after two good solid months of pre-season training and conditioning I was out for at least a week, letting my body heal itself. The injury occurred late in the match and luckily the referee called time soon after but I avoided the customary team talk after the match, going straight to the dressing room and eventually home to lay supine on the couch with ice under my leg.

I thought about injuries and about how lucky I was not to have sustained a serious one during the hundreds of games I had played, both in football and hurling for school, club, college and county. I had of course broken wrists and thumbs and fingers and torn ligaments and pulled muscles, but nothing that kept me sidelined for more than a few weeks. I had nearly lost my eye in the days when I did not wear a helmet when a broken hurl flew through the air and came within centimetres of piercing my eyeball. I had seen first-hand players getting their teeth knocked out, sustain concussions, break ribs and limbs, and tear cruciate ligaments, and a wave of gratitude suddenly enveloped me. I had done well; I was lucky and the longer I played I knew the chances of serious injury rose exponentially.

The training was getting harder too and I needed additional time to recover between games and training sessions. I was at least ten years older than the average age of the team and though I was maintaining my own personal fitness and playing levels I knew the clock was counting down. I was starting to fear being obliterated by an opponent, being shown up as a washed-up old lad who used to be good but really should have retired five years ago. I trained and pushed myself because of my fear of failure and my fear of letting the team, the players and management down.

That year I was ravaged with knocks and minor injuries and became a caricature of an out-of-shape middle-aged man competing with twenty-somethings. I had tendonitis in my left elbow and wrists, and striking the ball, particularly on my left side, led to involuntary whimpers of pain. I had cramps in my hips and muscle damage and tears along my calves and hamstrings. I would arrive thirty minutes before training officially started and endured the pain of rolling out my tired muscles, followed by light jogging and stretching to generate some blood flow. Training in winter was problematic; my old finger and wrist injuries would resurface and I would have to generously apply Deep Heat to my hands in order for my digits to flex sufficiently enough to catch a ball. I jealously looked on as my teammates bound from the dressing room without warmup or Deep Heat and drove sliotars from one side of the pitch to the other without fearing the potential consequences of injury.

I also began to look at my hurl and my gear in a different way too. I no longer had the burning desire to prove myself on the pitch to anyone any more. I had successes away from hurling in life, and I had overcome innumerable obstacles and had found a life companion who finally understood me. I wanted to do other things. I wanted to build my business, I wanted more time with the kids, I wanted to see how far I could push my speech in the real world and, not insignificantly, I wanted to be able to walk relatively upright the morning after playing a match.

During the time my hamstring healed I vowed to myself that if this really was my final year then I would give it everything I had. I wanted to be known as one of the best players the club had ever produced and I wanted the self-satisfaction that comes with knowing I had done absolutely everything I could to get the most out of myself. With a team sport there are so many variables that impinge upon individual performances that sometimes you are just not going to have the perfect match every time you step onto the field. But I wanted to walk away knowing that for one final year I was one of the best on the team and that when people talked about me the first thing they would say was that I was a good hurler, crucial to the team and a real leader, rather than someone who struggled with a stammer.

My club, Scoil Uí Chonaill, had given me so much, I wanted to do something on the field to acknowledge and repay the debt I owed. Playing for my club allowed me to play for and captain DCU and ultimately play for the county. I had played with and gotten to know an array of personalities and individuals who would remain close and important to me forever. I always felt proud and humbled when I wore my club colours, even during the bleak and lean years when we were not successful. I would remember the players who went before me, who at that time managed and coached me, and the teachers in the school who spent their lunch hours and after-school free time teaching me how to hurl and to kick a football. It was important for me to perform on the field for my last year because I wanted to leave on my own terms. I did not want to be forced away from the game through injury or unfortunate circumstance or from being dropped from the team by performing well below my best.

You can have the best intentions in the world to have a great year but invariably I was lucky too in that the players immediately around me – full-back, centre-back, left half-back and goalkeeper – had outstanding playing years too. I had the experience to know when to run, when to conserve my energy and when to deliver a pass or strike it long. I relied upon the players around me to sometimes cover my own man (as well as their own) as long as I was available to them when they were in trouble too. Conor Coady, Danny Mottram, Adam

Wilson and I played in the same positions for almost the entire year and match after match we performed as a solid unit, keeping the opposition forwards out and delivering balls into our own forward line. We talked continuously throughout the year during and after matches about providing the right cover for the goalkeeper and about how to prevent easy goals and minimise errors. These guys were coming into their hurling primes and they were vastly fitter and stronger than me; I benefitted hugely from playing beside them that final year.

The team began to generate momentum as we won games that in previous years we would have lost due to inexperience, lack of confidence or pure bad luck. The team was collectively very fit and the younger players who had for so long been naive and unsure of themselves blossomed into hardened club hurlers, ready to put their bodies on the line for the club and to win the all-important next ball.

That year was unusual too in that we played against very strong opposition that were not in our league. We played Glenmore, the Kilkenny county champions, in a Leinster club competition on a wet and dour day in Clontarf and we were heavily beaten. They had serious performers in their three Kilkenny senior players and really it was men against boys but looking back it was great to say you had marked a then current All-Star and Kilkenny player on your home pitch at the age of 40.

We reached the county final too and played against a strong Cuala side. It was to be my very last game playing in Parnell Park. Astrid came to see the match and I was very emotional at the final whistle. I had played and trained there so often with the club and the county and I knew I would never play there again. I had played well and won a lot of my personal battles that day and had no regrets. Cuala were a better side and deserved their victory. I stayed around on the pitch and watched the Cuala guys enjoy their moment as Astrid approached me, held my hand and congratulated me on my last time in Parnell Park. It had been a great occasion with lots of supporters from both clubs there and a special atmosphere. I had had a few rough times in Parnell Park with the Dubs in the past but hopefully I will see my children play there in the future and they will have more successful times than I did.

The final match at home would decide who would get promoted and it was between ourselves and our closest rivals and neighbours, Clontarf.

I tend to try not to think about matches until the time comes to actually play them. I learned from my experiences playing for Dublin not to overthink too much about performance because my mind catastrophises every scenario and invariably I have the mental image of me fluffing a clearance or catch indelibly imprinted on my mind. I had played so many matches in my time that I knew I could handle any consequence or occasion that would crop up unplanned in a match. I knew how to adapt. However, I was struggling to relinquish the negative thoughts that came unexpectedly with this match. Whatever the outcome or level of personal performance success achieved, I was done, I was finished, and yet I felt that one poor match would destroy the perception that I had had a good year and would inevitably leave my reputation tarnished in the club. I built it up as something hugely significant. For the first time since playing for Dublin I felt genuinely nervous about a match, about letting the team down and having to retire in a manner that I knew I would regret forever.

I had used visualisation techniques many times as part of my recovery from stammering. I used to hear and feel myself speak with power before a support group meeting or presentation. I tried to recapture that emotion, that feeling when you are in a moment where you are totally in control, in command and untouchable. That's what I had to do when thinking about that match. I replayed images of myself lifting the ball correctly, hand-passing to Conor, turning and striking on my left side and mentally preparing myself for being tired, drained and exhausted but having the will to drive on and win the next ball.

The match was played in late October; the pitch was heavy and sodden and probably suited backs more than forwards. I was delighted with the conditions; it would slow the ball coming into their forwards and give us backs the opportunity to get a hand or hurl in, to disrupt their primary possession and spoil the play. When primary possession is not won then it is an even contest and invariably whoever wants it the most will win out on the day. We had been playing well running up to the match and I was personally confident, but during the warmup and team talk I felt we were a little muted and over-dismissive of the challenge that Clontarf presented. The first half went well for me personally: there were lots of breaking balls to clear into our forwards and the boys immediately around my position in corner-back were keeping their respective men subdued. I had taken a few painkillers before the match due to the tendonitis in my wrist and for the first time in a long time I could strike the ball pain-free. Clontarf doggedly kept chipping away and there was not much between us at half-time. I remember walking over to the sideline thinking, I have to say something here. We are not motivated enough. This is my last game. These guys have years left to play and the next thirty minutes are my last. I suddenly felt myself become emotional and angry with how certain players had not been performing and indicated to the manager that I would like to say a few words to the team when he had completed his half-time instructions and talk.

I rarely speak at any length at half-time, not because of the stammer, just because I feel the captain should speak and retain command and frequently when too many players step forward and speak it degenerates into a screaming match.

When it was my turn to speak, I looked up to each player and stated that the performance was not good enough. I stated clearly and factually that we would not be losing today and I pointed directly at a number of players who although they had performed heroics all year were not playing well that day. I demanded more from these players simply because I knew they would deliver when the time came.

From the moment the referee blew his whistle those particular players I had addressed at half-time all raised their games to another level. They did the basics well and were full of industry and endeavour. All the players were spurred on by the example of these players and slowly we extended our lead. With fifteen minutes to go I ran to collect a ball from the sideline when I felt a sharp stabbing pain in my right hamstring and knew immediately it was torn. I bent down gingerly and delivered the ball up the line, cursing my body and hoping that the ball would not go near my wing for the rest of the match. Fortunately, our forwards did a great job of keeping the ball in their half and I spent the rest of the match stolidly limping after my man, counting down the seconds. When the whistle sounded I jumped, threw my hurl and helmet in the air and embraced the player nearest to me. I forgot the pain in my hamstring and sequentially jumped into and out of the arms of every player on the team. I was so relieved that collectively we had won but also personally that I had achieved what I had set out to achieve ten months previously. I had overcome my fragile body and ended my career after giving everything I had and with no regrets, with guys I had seen growing up before my eyes and with a management team who had known me since I was eight years old.

The following January I was awarded the Player of the Year at the club's award ceremony in Clontarf Castle and I chatted and mingled with people in the club whom I had known all my life. I was especially grateful to the players and management who had secured promotion and had soldiered with me for so long. It was time now for me to give something more tangible back to the club. I am currently involved in coaching and co-managing my son's football and hurling teams and am an avid supporter of my daughter who plays football and camogie too with the club. The first time I saw my son wear the club colours I was transported back to the early 1980s when our jerseys were not as sophisticated, comfortable or well-fitting as they ones they have now. But the crest is the same and I hope that both of my children get the same enjoyment and satisfaction as I did playing and as I currently do from being involved in coaching and management.

16

My Mental Health

Stammering affects 1 per cent of the population and I would hazard a guess and state that a good percentage of stammerers have at least thought about suicide at some stage. This is a depressing thought and demonstrates the supreme mental pressure and anxiety experienced by someone who stammers. Throughout my life I always knew I was hypersensitive: to sniggering sideways glances as I blocked on words or to perceived criticism of my hurling performances. In those immediate moments I recognised the imperceptible, unintentional slights even when there was none intended. My mind created challenges and anxieties by its own volition and loved to ruminate all through the night on why that teacher asked me to read that particular line of prose with all my feared words and sounds in it. How did he know I was struggling with 's' sounds lately? He purposely wants me to appear like an incoherent fool in class!

If I could distil down to a fine essence what state my mental health is, I would say that I 'feel' all the time. Emotions flood my nervous system at a constant and unhindered rate. I am always feeling something. Happiness, sadness, shame, fear, guilt, rage. But these feelings are given superhuman credence by the way my mind works. There is no generic baseline level of happiness or self-satisfaction; there is only absolute euphoria. There is no tolerable, resigned-to-the-fact state of general sadness. There is only depression and the possibilities presented by suicide. Anger is replaced by rage and apprehension is trumped by sheer pain-inducing terror. Guilt follows anger after I inevitably make an emotional outburst, frequently to a loved one, which then transcends into self-loathing and thoughts of self-harm. The feelings and emotions are fleeting, however, and when tears of frustration stream down my face another counter-emotion invites itself into my unstable psyche and I begin the analytical process of trying to rationalise what exactly happened to cause me to feel this way and what can I do next time to manage such feelings.

Sometimes, and I know this sounds contradictory for someone who stammers, I can say things that I do not mean. I say things to hurt, to maim, to cleave and to cause offence. My feelings, emotions and heart are not engaged to my speaking process during these times but it is the only outlet I have to vent those feelings that have invaded me. If someone really means something to me, if they are important in my life, then there is a good chance that I have said something to them that will make them hate me or at least want to punch me in the face. I have a fear of abandonment but I might say things that make you want to leave. Yes, I know this is not logical or rational or educated or measured; it is emotive, it is prehistoric, base-level emotional torture but I cannot help it. In fact, I often wonder what I would be like with no stammer. Imagine if I was more garrulous, more confident about speaking. The stammer has put an unintentional and much-maligned dam on my verbal outbursts that has probably ensured that I still have a handful of meaningful relationships in my life.

My mind makes small problems grow. I find the daily mundane, repetitive tasks of living Herculean trials that I find difficult to overcome. The car has broken down. That single seemingly innocuous problem will spark a series of emotional and mental outbursts that take every neuron in my brain to try to regulate my emotions and not to crumple me into a heap on the floor and wait for Astrid to sort it out. And if she doesn't sort it out soon, I won't be afraid to tell her and I will feel guilty for my reaction and my over-reliance on her when realistically the problem could be quite easily solved if my mind could simply focus on the task at hand rather than create a dystopian, life-threatening scenario where my daily routine had to be disturbed.

On the evening of the argument with Astrid, I am certain that if there had been a knife or razorblade in my room then I would have ended my life. I am as certain of this as of the fact that the debits and credits must agree while preparing a trial balance. In coming to terms with my reaction and trying to rationalise to myself how I could go from disagreeing with my partner to wanting to end my life, I not only had to take a long and revealing look at the way I react to certain stimuli but also cast my mind back to when my father used to bang his head against the wall and unequivocally determine that what my father and I did were wrong, irrational, over-emotional and destructive to not only myself but also to my relationship with everyone in my family. This incident was the catalyst for me to seriously think about my mental health.

During my employment years, I had difficulty in holding down a full-time job. I understand that stammering played a huge role too in how I performed and communicated in any position but my mental state also had a huge influence as to why I never truly felt comfortable or contented walking into work, for any job that I ever undertook. Certain people or instances or work practices could annoy me and I would focus all my attention on those issues, ignoring the more bearable and perhaps even enjoyable components of a paid position. My confidence and ego were always fragile too. Any impending deadlines would loom ominously over me for days and weeks and they would germinate self-imposed pressures and stresses that would perpetually dominate my free-time thoughts, inevitably ruining my day off/weekend/week off in the process. If my performance reports were not exemplary I would be devastated and even if they were I would feel I was being lied to, or manipulated, praised just enough to placate me and motivate me to push myself to another level at the same time. I became impulsive, threatening to leave, greeting Astrid with the ominous warning every morning at breakfast that today is finally the day when I hand in my notice. Of course I never had anything lined up or planned or in the pipeline but I thought we could always manage and maybe if things got tight we could sleep rough and rob all-night supermarkets for food and supplies. Yes, yes, I know this doesn't make sense to you; it certainly doesn't make sense to me but you see my emotions ran riot over all logical thought in my head. It took every ounce of Astrid's Germanic brain to temper my impulsiveness, persuade me to at least get through the day without offending someone (generally someone in a more senior position than me) and go through the motions for that all-important payday at the end of the month.

Looking back, I can pinpoint the reason for most of my failed relationships and unsurprisingly it was me. In fairness though it is hard to sustain a relationship when you hate yourself to such an extent that you starve yourself and where your confidence levels and your own self-esteem fluctuate as wildly as the weather. I also never knew who I really was. I didn't know if I was confident or a nice guy, or a moody guy, or an angry guy or an unlucky guy or someone who always saw the worst in every person and situation. I remember not speaking at my wedding – my stammer was too severe at the time – but I distinctly remember the extent of damage that one act of avoidance did to my consciousness. I absolutely loathed myself. I managed to trick my mind into thinking that I was protecting everyone else's feelings by not talking but to make no effort at all, no signal to acknowledge my wife, her family or anything that we had as a couple, sickened me. But the worst thing is that there are hundreds of situations in my life where I avoided, where I feigned ignorance, gave the wrong name, address, age, job title, car registration, child's name, all ostensibly because of my stammer but truly out of cowardice. That deeply ingrained damage to my mental health caused by my stammer has subsequently impeded the progress of my recovery from stammering and also enhanced the severity of my mental health issues. Having thought about it long and hard, the only way back, the only redemption, is to live the rest of my life not avoiding, even if I fail I succeed, even if I have a go, try, try and speak even when costal breathing, when my tools and technique abandon me. The repercussions of not trying are simply too severe to entertain.

My mother always said that I was a 'worrier', someone who 'takes things to heart' and 'thinks too much'. I have no problem with that prognosis. I always recognised that my mind was constantly working and, in particular, actively finding ways to worry. It is as if worrying is my natural default mental position. I often say to Astrid I would love just to be relaxed and I mean totally relaxed with my mind blank. Since I stopped hurling those moments are difficult to cultivate and hard to obtain. When you are hurling well, and playing well in a game, you are thinking only about the next ball, the next play, the strength of your grip on the handle of the hurley and not about the daily routine issues that have enveloped your days and nights for the past week. That is what hurling and sport gave me. A release. There was no talking involved, no demonstration of technical accounting knowledge, no arguments with a loved one and no guilt after for saying or in my case for not saying how you really felt. I miss that about hurling but in the later years that was poisoned too. Before games I would become nervous, visualise situations where I would fluff a strike or pick-up. My man has scored and I would be trailing in his wake as the net bulges. It took huge amounts of mental strength to try to replace those damaging images with positive ones.

Stress has become a recurring issue in my life simply because my mind has deemed it another of my natural states. Speaking and all issues relating to speaking create a certain stress in my life and so by the very fact that you have to speak and speak frequently in order to make a living and live your life there are more instances of stress in my life than I can handle naturally. The feeling I also have is that I live my life like it is the last ten minutes of a very important match. The risk of failure and promise of success are very evenly balanced and the time allowed for important decisions to be made has vanished. Everything must be done now, this minute, and at an electric pace. Instantly. No time to think about the consequences, the what-ifs, the end game. I feel rushed in everything I do. Sometimes I see a look of impatience in my listeners' eyes when I am speaking to them using my technique. I self-manifest time pressures in work simply because that is the way my mind works. I don't understand it. It just happens. I am always on edge, filled with anger and regret that I cannot regulate my emotions to a level where I can lay my head on my bed at night and say to myself 'today was a good day.'

Being with Astrid helps. Then, of course, me being me, being on my own also helps. Remedies and reliefs can be as ambiguous and unexpected as my triggers. Sometimes I don't know what will help my mental state; sometimes I just do things and they work or they make me worse and then it is a matter of going back to basics, thinking about the other rough times in my life and about the ways I overcame them. How did I do it back then? Will it work again?

After I retired from hurling, I used to go back to the hurling wall and perform my standard drills. Soon the pain would return to my elbow and wrists and I would have to call it a day. Sometimes I would run a few miles, listen to my music or an interesting podcast and that would work. Other days I would criticise myself for my lack of fitness and how in the past my time to run that distance would have been half. The curse of trying to resurrect past glories. I would read a lot, listen to audiobooks and try to calm my mind before bed. I listen to Conan Doyle a lot simply because my father introduced me to Sherlock Holmes as a boy and we used to watch the television series together in between shouting matches. I try to eat fairly clean and go the gym and once again try to regain the physique I had when I was 21. No use. The ship has sailed there. I listen to REM, the Cure, the Smiths and the 90s' classics that blared from wall-mounted speakers in every university bar we invaded during the DCU years. I try to be a good dad and good partner and try to recognise when I have hurt someone and endeavour not to do it again. I work on my speech and go to the odd McGuire meeting or do my breathing and visualise myself overcoming my stammer, speaking well and commanding a room. I try not to think about the headaches and migraines and medication or my father and the bad times. I try to enjoy some or a single part of a day. I look forward to my time with the kids and enjoy coaching and watching their matches. I've read books about cycling around the world and I want to try that, maybe when the kids are grown up. Just the thought of getting on a bike and going, simply going and not looking back, that appeals to me.

I just get on with things, reluctantly, begrudgingly, needing Astrid's encouragement and, sometimes, stern warnings. There is no worthwhile alternative.

17

Answers

The first few sessions with the psychologist were difficult because they required me to speak at length about my childhood, my stammer and my recent emotional problems rather than discussing how I was going to regulate my emotions and take back control over my life. Much like my introduction to the McGuire Programme, I wanted answers immediately.

She agreed that I definitely had serious mental health issues and she bluntly explained that this would be a long-term battle which required ongoing sessions with her and careful monitoring of my emotions when I left the room. Ideally, I would have to track my emotions on a daily basis, carefully document any emotional outbursts and thereby monitor my progress over time.

Most of the sessions were with Astrid present as the psychologist felt it was important that not only Astrid's mental health was monitored too given that invariably she was on the receiving end of my outbursts but that also she understood how my mind operated and how my emotions governed my behaviours in times of distress. The sessions were scheduled to ensure I was able to discuss the events of the past week and pinpoint my emotional triggers and formulate strategies for me to regulate my emotions. I was experiencing intense emotions every day. The feelings invariably centred on my children and my separation anxiety.

Eventually, as the sessions progressed, coupled with my own intensive research and readings, I developed a number of very practical tools to try to regulate my emotions. During these emotional periods, thoughts about running away, leaving my job and harming myself would suffocate my rational mind. I had not come to terms with the trauma I had experienced as a child, I had not fully accepted myself as a stammerer (even after the McGuire Programme) and the divorce was still very raw.

My mind was filled with various thoughts about leaving Ireland, trying to do something about my stammer, changing my job (again), dealing with the necessary ongoing communications with my ex-wife, money and trying to build a future with Astrid.

The psychologist recommended I start to practice daily mindfulness as a means of quieting my mind and giving me some relief from the constant barrage of negativity that occupied my mind. Mindfulness is simply paying extra attention to something on purpose and ensuring you are only thinking in the present moment. Every action can be a mindful one, even sitting on a chair. You focus your mind to think about the feel of the chair on your legs and backside, how comfortable it is, how deep you are sinking into the cushions, the feel of the armrests on your forearms, etc. I immediately recognised the connection to stammering and the various methods I was taught to deal with a feared word or sound. I was learning new tools and techniques which could be employed to assist with the mental issues I was having.

The psychologist also recognised that there was immense pressure in my life, especially after dealing with all the legal issues associated with the divorce. The issue of dealing with stress is called distress tolerance. This is simply engaging in another more positive activity when stress and the associated negative thoughts envelope your mind. I had noticed over time that my tolerance for daily stress had diminished since the divorce and that every event out of the ordinary or every perceived slight from Astrid would cause me immense emotional discomfort. I appeared to have lost the ability to deal maturely with any level of stress in my life. The specific skill I was going to have to learn was to acknowledge the presence of stress and deal with it in a more positive fashion (as opposed to sticking pens in my arm). I recognised I could go running, listen to music or sit down and talk to Astrid when I felt the approach of heightened stress levels in my body.

I experienced conflicting heightened emotions. I recognised those variances myself many times when I became angry with myself or Astrid and then a couple of minutes later my heightened emotions would subside and stabilise. I recognised that my emotions would only stay heightened for a relatively short period of time, especially my anger. I would have to adopt a strategy of taking myself out of that position or emotion for a few minutes in order for my emotions to dissolve. This was going to take a huge amount of work and self-control.

Finally, the psychologist encouraged me to review key relationships in my life and especially those with my father, my family and best friends. I had a couple of really good friends from the McGuire Programme whom I had lost touch with over the years. I decided to rekindle those friendships as a means of establishing a stronger support network for my mental health, increasing my own self-worth and to generally have more positive people in my life.

Seeing the psychologist provided some answers as to why I always felt different growing up and why I appear to struggle more through life as opposed to 'normal' people. I cannot shake off disappointments quick enough, daily challenges appear insurmountable and my moods and emotions escalate and plummet instantaneously and from triggers as innocuous as words, looks from people, comments and innocent actions. The whole process is exhausting and frustrating but has given me some comfort that I am not the useless incompetent person I labelled myself throughout my life due to my inability to speak. I just feel 'differently'. My emotions overrun my rational mind. Whereas bouts of depression can last for many months and years for some people, for me they can last an hour, an afternoon or a day and then subside to an unsustainable elated feeling as I perceive that I have finally overcome that particular low in my life, until another comes along to drag me down again.

The process of emotional stabilisation and regulation is definitely going to be a long-term project. It is something I am going to have to focus and work on for the rest of my life. I approach it the same way I have my ongoing recovery from stammering, from initial self-acceptance (again, still an ongoing process), attaining key requisite knowledge and experience, and implementing the skills and experiences learned in order to live each day progressively more fulfilled and less self-destructive. Every day I experience triggers that threaten to destabilise my emotions but I am slowly coming to terms with dealing with implementing tools, like mindfulness and meditation, and soon, if diligently applied, they will become automatic.

I feel I have made huge strides in recent months with losing the vast majority of my negative stammering mentality. I have lost most pre-event anxiety through a combination of mindfulness, use of McGuire techniques and of course knowing that I have overcome various difficult challenges in my life which has given me enormous positive reinforcement to draw from. John Harrison said in his book that he lost all the psychological issues connected with stammering way before he lost the physical manifestations. That is significant because once the mental approach is right and there is no psychological scarring from stammering then I believe the stammer will simply dissolve – it has no fuel to sustain it. I still practice and I still complete my daily breathing exercises, rather for its more holistic, relaxing attributes now than its targeted specific intent of warming up my costal diaphragm. My focus now is on communication rather than perfect physical speech production. I am happy now to convey my message and my intent, to be able to get my point across to my listener and if that is achieved with less than perfect technique then I am very satisfied with that outcome. For so many years I simply could not communicate and then when I acquired new tools and techniques I used to berate myself for not employing those techniques to absolute perfection. I was creating additional negative consequences in my mind for incorrect communication when instead I should have been applauding myself for non-avoidance in the first place. I speak now, more automatically than ever, sometimes with technique, sometimes without, depending on my own confidence levels and my sensitivity indifference levels. The most important thing I believe is that I communicate, rather than speak, and I communicate now when I feel I have something worthy to contribute. It took me over 40 years to come to this realisation.

My past relationships were tumultuous and traumatic primarily due to my mental health and my stammer. I have no such excuses now. I have a greater understanding now through therapy and research of how my mind and emotions work and I don't want to blow it again. All through therapy I thought about my family, my childhood and the dominating influence my father had on the household and in particular me. It is only when raising children yourself you come to realise how difficult that task really is. We grew up in claustrophobic conditions; my parents constantly worried about finances and were consumed with raising their children the best they could. It was difficult for me but it was difficult for them too having to raise someone as hypersensitive as myself who simply did not know how to deal with any of the issues I began to face when I started school. My memories of my father have been hugely conflicted during the course of writing this book but as my awareness of my own condition developed through therapy, age and experience, I started to remember the good times with my father as opposed to the destructive ones. There were times in my life, very rarely, when I asked him directly for his prescient advice and help and he always stood by my side. He sacrificed his own ambitions and desires and put everything he could into raising our family. He pushed and cajoled me into wanting to get the best from myself, both academically and through sport. He taught me the importance of hard work and self-discipline and shared his appetite for reading, knowledge and acuity with me. There were always books everywhere around the house when I was growing up and we never wanted for hot meals, shelter or moral guidance. We grew up in the north inner city of Dublin and were exposed to so much of the world and its possibilities through his knowledge and own experiences. He achieved this while experiencing his own mental health issues. It is only fair that I recognise his positive influence in my upbringing along with my mother's and my sisters' contributions. I am empathetic and entirely grateful for their collective influence and realise I could not have achieved the goals I had set out for myself at a young age without their help, guidance and advice.

In writing this final chapter, I wish there was a spectacularly triumphant ending, a resounding redemptive arc and a tangible solution to my stammering and mental and physical health issues.

There is not. There is only a burning realisation that life is sincerely what you make it and it is very difficult to make it on your own. I needed the support and encouragement of someone very special and understanding to help me define clearly what my problems were and to begin yet another journey toward problem recognition and management. I still get headaches, I still stutter, I still have bad thoughts but not to the same degree as when they afflicted me at their worst. I still push myself to speak and I recognise, perhaps not all the time, but with increasing frequency, when my emotions are starting to gain the upper hand. I try and I falter, recalibrate and go again. Maybe that is the theme of this book: getting good at falling down, and getting back up again.